The Royal Master by James Shirley

As it was Acted in the new Theater in Dublin: And Before the Right Honorable the Lord Deputie of Ireland, in the Castle.

James Shirley was born in London in September 1596.

His education was through a collection of England's finest establishments: Merchant Taylors' School, London, St John's College, Oxford, and St Catharine's College, Cambridge, where he took his B.A. degree in approximately 1618.

He first published in 1618, a poem entitled Echo, or the Unfortunate Lovers.

As with many artists of this period full details of his life and career are not recorded. Sources say that after graduating he became "a minister of God's word in or near St Albans." A conversion to the Catholic faith enabled him to become master of St Albans School from 1623–25.

He wrote his first play, Love Tricks, or the School of Complement, which was licensed on February 10th, 1625. From the given date it would seem he wrote this whilst at St Albans but, after its production, he moved to London and to live in Gray's Inn.

For the next two decades, he would write prolifically and with great quality, across a spectrum of thirty plays; through tragedies and comedies to tragicomedies as well as several books of poetry. Unfortunately, his talents were left to wither when Parliament passed the Puritan edict in 1642, forbidding all stage plays and closing the theatres.

Most of his early plays were performed by Queen Henrietta's Men, the acting company for which Shirley was engaged as house dramatist.

Shirley's sympathies lay with the King in battles with Parliament and he received marks of special favor from the Queen.

He made a bitter attack on William Prynne, who had attacked the stage in Histriomastix, and, when in 1634 a special masque was presented at Whitehall by the gentlemen of the Inns of Court as a practical reply to Prynne, Shirley wrote the text—The Triumph of Peace.

Shirley spent the years 1636 to 1640 in Ireland, under the patronage of the Earl of Kildare. Several of his plays were produced by his friend John Ogilby in Dublin in the first ever constructed Irish theatre; The Werburgh Street Theatre. During his years in Dublin he wrote The Doubtful Heir, The Royal Master, The Constant Maid, and St. Patrick for Ireland.

In his absence from London, Queen Henrietta's Men sold off a dozen of his plays to the stationers, who naturally, enough published them. When Shirley returned to London in 1640, he finished with the Queen Henrietta's company and his final plays in London were acted by the King's Men.

On the outbreak of the English Civil War Shirley served with the Earl of Newcastle. However when the King's fortunes began to decline he returned to London. There his friend Thomas Stanley gave him help and thereafter Shirley supported himself in the main by teaching and publishing some educational works under the Commonwealth. In addition to these he published during the period of dramatic eclipse four small volumes of poems and plays, in 1646, 1653, 1655, and 1659.

It is said that he was "a drudge" for John Ogilby in his translations of Homer's Iliad and the Odyssey, and survived into the reign of Charles II, but, though some of his comedies were revived, his days as a playwright were over.

His death, at age seventy, along with that of his wife, in 1666, is described as one of fright and exposure due to the Great Fire of London which had raged through parts of London from September 2nd to the 5th.

He was buried at St Giles in the Fields, in London, on October 29th, 1666.

Index of Contents
To the Right Honorable, George Earle of Kildare, Baron of Opbalie
DRAMATIS PERSONAE
SCENE - Naples, and Simphorosa's Country House
THE ROYAL MASTER
THE FIRST ACT
SCENE I - Naples – The Palace
SCENE II - Simphorosa's Country House
THE SECOND ACT
SCENE I - The Same
SCENE II - The Same – A Garden
THE THIRD ACT
SCENE I - Naples. A Part of the Palace
SCENE II - A Room in the Palace
SCENE III - Another Room in the Same.
THE FOURTH ACT
SCENE I - A Room in the Palace.
THE FIFTH ACT
SCENE I - Naples – A Room in the Palace.
SCENE II - Another Room in the Scene.
THE EPILOGUE
POEMS IN PRAISE OF JAMES SHIRLEY
To My Ingenious Friend, James Shirley, Upon His Royall Master by James Mervyn
On Mr. James Shirley's Royall Master by Fra. Butler
Upon Mr. James Shirley His Comedy, Cal'd The Royall Master by Drv. Cooper
On the Royall Master, to His Friend the Author by Ric. Belling
To My Deserving Friend Mr. James Shirley on His Royall Master by T.I.
To His Much Esteemed Friend Mr. James Shirley, on His Royall Master by W. Markham
To the Honour'd Author of the Royall Master by W. Smith
To His Worthy Friend the Author by John Ogleby Oglebye

To the Much Honoured, James Shirley Upon His Royall Master by John Jacson
On M. James Shirley His Royall Master by James Mervyn
JAMES SHIRLEY – A CONCISE BIBLIOGRAPHY

To the Right Honorable, George Earle of Kildare, Baron of Opbalie, and Primier Earle of the Kingdome of Ireland.

My Lord,

It was my happinesse being a stranger in this kingdome, to kisse your Lordships hands, to which your noblenesse, and my owne ambition encourag'd me, nor was it without justice to your name, to tender the first fruits of my observance to your Lordship, whom this Island acknowledgeth her first native Ornament and top branch of Honour. Be pleased now my most honorable Lord, since my Affaires in England hasten my departure, and prevent my personall attendance, that something of me may be honour to waite upon you in my absence, this Poeme; tis new, and never yet personated, but expected with the first, when the English Stage shall bee recovered from her long silence, and her now languishing scene changed into a welcome returne of wits and men; And when by the favour of the winds and Sea, I salute my Country againe, I shall report a story of the Jrish honour, and hold my selfe not meanely fortunate to have beene written and receiv'd

The humblest of your Lordships servants.
JAMES SHIRLEY.

DRAMATIS PERSONAE
King of Naples
Duke of Florence, suitor to Theodosia
Montalto, the king's favourite
Riviero, a Nobleman, banished from the Court, but returned in disguise, as theDuke's Secretary, under the name of Philoberto
Octavio, a young Courtier, son of Riviero
Andrugio, a Courtier, and friend to Riviero
Guido }
Aloiso } Attendants on the Court, and creatures of Montalto
Alexio }
Bombo, Secretary to Domitilla
Iacomo }
Pietro } Servants of Simphorosa
Courtiers, Petitioners, Servants, Attendants &c

Theodosia, the King's Sister
Simphorosa, a Noble widow
Domitilla, her Daughter
Ladies attending Theodosia

SCENE

Naples, and Simphorosa's Country House

THE FIRST ACT

SCENE I

Naples – The Palace.

Enter **KING of NAPLES**, the **DUKE of FLORENCE, MONTALTO, OCTAVIO, RIVIERO, ANDRUGIO, GUIDO, ALOISIO, ALEXIO.**

DUKE of FLORENCE
Y'Are great in all that's good.

KING of NAPLES
You shew the bounty
Of your opinion; my extent in all things
Is but to bid you welcome; you had a sister,
The envy of the Angels whilst she lived
Our Queene, now made their blest companion;
Should wee exempt those faire deserts dwell in you,
So much we owe her memory.

DUKE of FLORENCE
Pray no more.

RIVIERO
We must not be too open, truest friend,
Thy bosome is my Sanctuary.

ANDRUGIO
When it leaves
To be Religious for thy safety, may it
By an angry flame from heaven, be turnd to ashes.

DUKE of FLORENCE
Your nature is too soft; let not the mention
Of her that was my sister, and you Queene
Beget another sigh; she was long since blest;
Cesaria is in heaven; we are met for joyes;
You were not framed to be her Monument;
Sleepe let her ashes in the urne, conteines 'em.

KING of NAPLES.
I ha done.

[Enter **THEODOSIA, LADIES**.

DUKE of FLORENCE
Your sister.

KING of NAPLES.
Is all the treasure
Is left me sir, but cannot be too rich
For your acceptance.

DUKE of FLORENCE
All my wealth is summ'd
When shee does smile upon me, and her Character
In the full glory, when shee's nam'de your sister;
Are you not weary of a guest deare Madam?
Am I still welcome?

THEODOSIA
Sir wee are
All honour'd in your presence; and though not high
To your merit, yet your entertainement is,
As full of love, as nature can expresse
To a twin brother, more I dare presume,
You shall accuse your selfe, if you be lesse,
A Prince in Naples by free use of power,
Then your owne Florence.

DUKE of FLORENCE
Madam you must be
Lesse faire, and powerfull in tongue, if you
Expect I should be still a Prince; and yet
My ambition will be high, and glorious
Enough to be receiv'd your Graces servant;
For whom I should account my age no travell,
To have my pilgrimage rewarded with
Your faire eyes Madam, able to create
Another life and spirit in old Nature.

KING of NAPLES
How does Montalto like the Duke?

MONTALTO
Sir, Naples cannot study an addition
Of fame, beyond what this alliance will

Deserve in future story; the excesse
Of what is good, nay excellent in him
Would stocke a barren Province.

KING
Tis our happinesse.

MONTALTO
But 'tis not mine; for though I thus disguise
My face, and tongue, my heart is my owne friend,
And cannot wish my ambition supplanted
By any smooth chin'd Prince alive; my Lords—

ANDRUGIO
Look how they flock, and fawne upon his greatnes;
These are his creatures, by his power plac'd
So neare about the King, he can heare nothing
Of his great favorite, but what their flattery
And partiall tongues convey into his eare.

RIVIERO
Pitty so sweete a nature as the Kings
Should be abus'd by Parasites; but I may
In time dissolve these court mists, that so long
Have hung upon't, and render the Kings eyes
Free to distinguish objects, if there be
No witchcraft exerciz'd upon his senses.

1ST LADY
My Lord you are very pleasant.

OCTAVIO
Is it not
Becomming the discretion of a young
Courtier to observe times and methods; and when Madam
Are you for this match?

1ST LADY
What my Lord?

OCTAVIO
You wod not
Be sad at heart, to sleepe with such a bedfellow
As the Duke is?

2ND LADY
How my Lord?

OCTAVIO
Provided
Matrimony were not farre of; yet without it
There are some Ladies, would excuse their modestie,
And meete and thinke their fate at all adventures,
If no worse man would make their husband of
The honorable order of the night-cap.

1ST LADY
When will you marry my Lord?

OCTAVIO
I am young;
Yet when I am ripe to grapple with a maidenhead,
The Lord Montalto the great Court Patron
Will help me to a wife.

2ND LADY
You are bound to his Lordship.

OCTAVIO
And so I am Madam, if you knew all;
I have many obligations to his honour,
But there is one writ here, whose memory
Will keepe my soule awake.

KING of NAPLES
Andrugio—

GUIDO
I doe not like their conference.

MONTALTO
'Las he has no imployment in the state;
He waites like a dull cipher and I have
My spies upon him; if I finde him busie,
My power with the king shall soone transplant him,
Or force him like Riviero his old friend,
But of more braine and faction, to give up
His ghost abroad.

ALOISIO
'Twas just for your owne safety.

MONTALTO
This is an honest easy Nobleman,
Allowed to weare some Court formallity;
Walke on the tarres, picke his teeth, and stroake
Vpon a festivall some golden sentence

Out of his beard, for which the guard admire him,
And cry him up a Statesman; hee's sent off
When he is troublesome to a phlegmaticke clime
A dull Embassadour; no, that Duke, Guido,
Is all my feare, but I have contrived something
May rectifie my fate.

DUKE of FLORENCE
How much you honour me;
But you might spare all other entertainements
And bravery of Court; they may affect
My eyes with wonder, and obliege my just
Acknowledgement, but all their glorie's met
Into one height, hold no proportion
To inflame my heart, or more expresse my welcome
Then this your free grace Madam, and those hopes
That blesse my imagination from your favour.

THEODOSIA
I am but what my brothers love, and vertue
Will make me; but there's nothing that can move
With his consent, I shall not flee to obey.

MONTALTO
I had rather feede upon his heart;
You promis'd Sir the Duke to hunt this morning.

KING of NAPLES
I had forgot; will you be pleas'd to try
The pleasures of a Forrest.

DUKE of FLORENCE
Ile attend.

KING of NAPLES
Theodosia, you are not for that exercise Guido.

[Whispers and sends **GUIDO** off.

THEODOSIA
I wish all pleasures waite upon you;
My heart must covet your returne.

DUKE of FLORENCE
And mine,
To dwell for ever in so faire a bosom.

KING of NAPLES

To horse; the morning wasts.

MONTALTO
Some policie
Must cure this feare; my bold resolves are fixt;
I have made some attempts, and courted her,
But shee has not understood me; I must worke
By countermine and scatter into aire
His swelling hopes: Octavio—

[Exit.

OCTAVIO
My good Lord.

ANDRUGIO
Sir I present this Gentleman to kisse
Your hand; hee's the Dukes secretary, a Roman
Borne, and has a great ambition
To be knowne to you for your fathers sake,
With whom he did converse in Rome, and honour,
Till death concluded their acquaintance.

OCTAVIO
Sir,
Your love, and knowledge of my father will
Deserve you should be welcome to his sonne.

RIVIERO
He made me his companion many yeares;
No brothers were more chain'd in their affections.
He did impart much of his bosome to me.

OCTAVIO
You knew why he left Naples?

RIVIERO
He did trust me, with the cause my Lord, and every circumstance
The Kings minoritie, and Montaltoes power,
Gainst which no innocent could plead in Naples.

ANDRUGIO
Not to loud Sir; you may be heard.

RIVIERO
Your pardon.

OCTAVIO

Why should truth
Faint at the name of greatnesse? this Colossus
Montalto is but mortall sure; time has
Forgot to use his wings, or nature is
Unwilling I should grow to write full man,
To take revenge upon that polititian,
Our Protean favourite.

RIVIERO
It is my wonder
The King so strangely should continue this
Affection to Montalto.

OCTAVIO
There's some magicke in 't.

RIVIERO
Dare none complaine.

ANDRUGIO
His engines are so plac'd
None can approach the kings eare, at which hang
So many flatterers to infect it with
Montaltoes praise.

RIVIERO
Pray give me sir this boldnesse;
Hee that doth lift an Axe to strike the roote
Of any family, cannot be without
A thought to wound the branches; you were left.
By computation, but an Infant when
Your fathers discontents, and faction of
This Montalto made him forsake Naples,
Which added to your mothers death, the guard
And comforts of your life, were taken from you;
Having exprest this malice to your father,
A thousand wayes he might have sent you to
Another world, and taken off all feare
Of a revenge; how comes it that you live,
And visit Sir the Pallace with this freedome?

OCTAVIO
My Lord Andrugios knowledge of you Sir
Is my assurance of your faith.

ANDRUGIO
Ile give
You reasons at some opportunity

Not to repent your confidence.

OCTAVIO
You have
Supplied my fathel in your care of me.
I live? why I am this great Lords favorite,
Courted, his creatures are my honours
Companion to his pleasures.

RIVIERO
I observ'd
Some gestures very loving to your Lordship.

OCTAVIO
The King himselfe for his sake gracing me,
With title of his bed-chamber.

RIVIERO
Tis stange;
This newes will coole my resolution.

ANDRUGIO
Tis truth he doth ingage him to all favours.

RIVIERO
Tis not impossible he may be honest.

OCTAVIO
And meane so; but my soule cannot be brib'd
So easily to prostrate my owne justice
And leave my fathers ashes unreveng'd
Which in my eare groane from beneath the Marble
To keepe my thoughts awake.

ANDRUGIO
We may suspect
This is to catch applause a tricke to winne
Upon the people who did love Riviero
And mourne his fate.

OCTAVIO
How ever I have art
To keepe my breast close, and accept his flatteries,
Can complement, and with officious bend
Thanke his high favours, weare a face of mirth
And prattle with the Ladies as if all
The businesse I came into the world for,
Were but to talke and dance, and goe a feasting.

RIVIERO
I must presume, you want no counsell from
My Lord who loved your father, how to manage
Your selfe to best advantage of your name
And honour; unto both I am a servant.

ANDRUGIO
My Lord Montalto may expect you Sir.

RIVIERO
It is not safe we be observ'd too much.

OCTAVIO
My Lord you have begun a favour by
The acquaintance of this Gentleman; I will
Hope to salute him often by your meanes;
You shall not meete a heart more prompt to bid
You welcome Sir.

RIVIERO
You too much grace your servant;
I shall present a trouble.

OCTAVIO
Come my Lord.

[Exit.

RIVIERO
Montaltoes change hath staggard me already;
These favours may be hearty to Octavio,
And argument of penitence; Ile observe
And sift his close heart; if it prove unsound,
He whets revenge to make the deeper wound

[Exit.

SCENE II

Simphorosa's Country House

[Enter **GUIDO**, **BOMBO**.

GUIDO
I would speake with your Lady Sir.

BOMBO
You may.

GUIDO
Direct me.

BOMBO
With which of my Ladies.

GUIDO
With both, or one.

BOMBO
I serve the daughter.

GUIDO
I would speake with her.

BOMBO
Shee is—I know not where.

GUIDO
What Coxcombe's this.

[Enter **IACAMO**.

GUIDO
Dost heare friend, I would speake with my Lady Simphorosa.

IACAMO
This way and please your Lordship.

GUIDO
Stay preethe; what fellowe's that?

IACAMO
A servant of my Ladies.

GUIDO
Is he mad?

IACAMO
A little phantasticke, but very harmelesse,
And makes my Ladies merry; my young Madam
Domitilla calls him her secretary for sport
And wonder of his good parts.

GUIDO
What are they?

IACAMO
He can neither write nor reade.

GUIDO
An excellent Secretary.

IACAMO
But he has beene much given to 't,
To reading, till much poring night and day
Made him booke blinde; and defying spectacles,
He walkes and thinkes he is wise, and talkes upon
His old stocke.

GUIDO
Preethe acquaint my Lady

[Exit **IACOMO**.

—'ith meane time
Ile have more dialogue with him;
Save you Sir.

BOMBO
Save your selfe Sir; you are I tak't a Courtier.

GUIDO
And you my Ladies Secretary.

BOMBO
I am so.

GUIDO
I heare you are an understanding Secretary.

BOMBO
Tis so, I am; how came you by that knowledge.

GUIDO
We have your same at Court Sir.

BOMBO
Can you reade?

GUIDO

I heare you cannot.

BOMBO
Right.

GUIDO
Nor write.

BOMBO
Tis true.

GUIDO
What make you with a booke? ha this is Euclid.

BOMBO
Euclid; it may be so.

GUIDO
Why these are Mathematickes.

BOMBO
I have a Chest full of them in my custody;
They were my old Lords, gray when I tooke charge on 'em
But now looke spruce and young; there's something in 'em.

GUIDO
What in the name of ignorance dost thou doe with 'em.

BOMBO
I am excellent at turning over leaves,
By which I keepe the wormes away.

GUIDO
Most learnedly.

BOMBO
I learnt it of my Ladies Chaplaine Sir;
Men are not always bound to understand
Their Library; but to omit learning,
Not now consider'd by wise men, what is
Your businesse here I pray?

GUIDO
It does concerne
Your selfe; the King has heard of your good parts.

BOMBO
Sir, as you love me say you saw me not;

I knew I should one time or other be
Found out for state imployments; heer's my Lady.

[Going.

[Enter **SIMPHOROSA, DOMITILLA,**

I must obscure my selfe.

[**GUIDO** converses apart with **SIMPHOROSA**.

DOMITILLA
Why how now Secretary,
Whether so fast.

BOMBO
You little thinke.

DOMITILLA
What preethe.

BOMBO
Nor ever would beleeve; but tis not my fault
If the King come in person, Ile not be seene.

DOMITILLA
The King.

BOMBO
Few words; there's one I know him not
If little better then a spy upon me;
If you looke not to me I am gone.

[Exit.

DOMITILLA
So it seemes.

SIMPHOROSA
How? dine to day with us.

GUIDO
Such is his royall pleasure;
He is now hunting with the Duke, whom he
Intends to make your guest too.

SIMPHOROSA
My Lord I am not us'd to entertainements,

Nor is my house sit for so great a presence;
To avoide a storme they might obey
Necessity, and take it for some shelter,
But in so calme a day.

GUIDO
Madam although
You please to undervalew what's your owne,
The King despaires not you will bid him welcome;
You have no narrow dwelling, and he knowes
Your heart is spacious like your fortunes Madam;
Princes doe honour when they come upon
Their subjects invitation, but they love
Where they invite themselves.

SIMPHOROSA
My duty is
To meete that interpretation, though the newes
Come unexpected; now it will my Lord
Become me to be thrifty of the minute,
Their persons being so neare; you will excuse
If so short summons doe expect my care
To entertaine 'em; my good Lord you have honor'd me.

GUIDO
Tis service I am bound to.

[Exit **SIMPHOROSA**.

DOMITILLA
Pray my Lord.
In your opinion, what should moove the King
To invite himselfe our guest, and bring the Duke
Along with him; he us'd not to retire
From hunting with this ceremony.

GUIDO
Princes
Are like the windes, and not to be examin'd
Where they will breath their favours.

DOMITILLA
Tis confest
An honour to us, and I hope you'le pardon
A womans curiositie.

GUIDO
Shall I

Deliver my opinion; while the King
In entertainement of the Duke is shewing
The pleasures and the glories of his kingdome
He cannot hide, that which his Naples boasteth,
Her greatest ornament your beauty Madam.

DOMITILLA
I thanke your Lordship; I may now beleeve
The court's remooving hither; yet this language
Might doe you service to some other Lady
And I release it willingly; your complements
I know my Lord are much worse for wearing

GUIDO
You rather will beleeve your selfe worth praise
Then heare it; though we call it modesty,
It growes from some thing like a womans pride;
But it becomes you Madam; I take leave;
My service to your noble Lady mother.

[Exit **GUIDO**.

DOMITILLA
Mine shall attend your Lordship.

[Enter **SIMPHOROSA**.

SIMPHOROSA
Now Domitilla, is my Lord gone?

DOMITILLA
Yes Madam.

SIMPHOROSA
I expected not
These guests to day, they'le take us unprepard.

DOMITILLA
Not with our hearts to serve 'em, and their goodnes
Will excuse other want.

SIMPHOROSA
I know not daughter,
But I could wish rather to enjoy our selves,
Not for the cost, those thoughts are still beneath me.

DOMITILLA
You have cause to feare I hope y'are troubled.

SIMPHOROSA
For thy sake Domitilla.

DOMITILLA
Mine deare Madam.

SIMPHOROSA
It was for thee I chose this quiet life
Vpon thy fathers death, and left the court;
Thou art all my care, sole heire to all my fortunes,
Which I should see unwillingly bestowed.
On some gay prodigall.

DOMITILLA
I cannot teach
Your meaning.

SIMPHOROSA
By some hastie marriage.

DOMITILLA
You would have me live a Virgin; a lesse fortune
Would serve me for a Nunne.

SIMPHOROSA
Tis not my thought;
Thou art young and faire and though I doe not
Suspect thy minde, thus farre bred up to vertue,
I would not have it tempted but reservde
For a most noble choise, wherein should meet
My care and thy obedience.

DOMITILLA
Y'are my mother,
And have so farre by your example taught me,
I Shall not neede the precepts of your vertue,
And let no thought of me take from your cheerefulnesse
To entertaine the King; we owe him duty,
And that charme wo'not hurt us.

SIMPHOROSA
This does please me.

DOMITILLA
It shall be still my study.

SIMPHOROSA

I must see
How they prepare, things may want method else.

[Exit **SIMPHOROSA**.

[Enter **OCTAVIO**.

OCTAVIO
I kisse your faire hand Madam Domitilla;
The King and Duke and all the jolly hunters
With appetites as fierce as their owne hounds,
Will be here presently.

DOMITILLA
I hope they will not
Devoure us my good Lord.

OCTAVIO
But I would sit and feast and feed mine eyes
With Domitillaes beauty.

DOMITILLA
So my Lord; here was a gentleman
You could not choose but meete him spake your dialect;
I have forgot his name, but he was some
Great Lord.

OCTAVIO
Fye what a ignorance you live in,
Not to be perfect in a great Lords name;
There are few Ladies live with us but know
The very Pages; leave this darkenesse Madam▪
And shine in your owne sphere, where every starre
Hath his due adoration.

DOMITILLA
Where?

OCTAVIO
The Court
Confine such beauty to a Countrey house!
Live among Hindes, and thicke skind fellowes that
Make faces, and will hop a furlong backe
To finde the tother leg they threw away
To shew their reverence; with things that squat
When they should make a curtsey; to Court Madam,
And live not thus for shame, the second part
Of a fond Anchorite; we can distinguish

Of beauty there, and wonder without spectacles,
Write Volumes of your praise, and tell the world
How envious diamonds, cause they could not
Reach to the lusture of your eyes dissolv'd
To angry teares; the Roses droope, and gathering
Their leaves together, seeme to chide their blushes
That they must yeeld your cheeke the victory:
The Lillies when they are censur'd for comparing
With your more cleare and native purity
Want white to doe their pennance in.

DOMITILLA
So, so;
Have you done now my young poeticke Lord.

OCTAVIO
There will be no end Madam of your praises.

DOMITILLA
And to no end you have spent all this breath;
Allow all this were wit, that some did thinke us
The creatures they commend (and those whom love
Hath curst into Idolatry and verse
May perhaps die so) wee doe know our selves
That we are no such things.

OCTAVIO
Ist possible.

DOMITILLA
And laugh at your Chimeraes.

OCTAVIO
Y'are the wiser.

DOMITILLA
If this be your court practise, let me dwell
With truth and plaine simplicity.

OCTAVIO
If I
Might have my choyse, I would live with you Madam▪
A neighbour to this innocence; your mother.

[Enter **SIMPHOROSA**.

SIMPHOROSA
The king is come already.

[Enter **KING of NAPLES, DUKE of FLORENCE, MONTALTO, GUIDO, ALOISIO, ALEXIO.**

KING of NAPLES
Madam though you are
So unkinde as not to see the court sometime,
The court is come to visit you.

SIMPHOROSA
You have
Humbled your selfe too much to doe us honour.

KING of NAPLES
The Duke of Florence.

SIMPHOROSA
Tis a blessing that
My roofe can boast so great a guest.

KING of NAPLES
Her daughter
Worth your salute.

DUKE of FLORENCE
Shee is worth a world my Lord,
What is that Ladies name?

MONTALTO
In this you most
Appeare a stranger; shee is the glory
Of Naples, for her person and her vertues
That dwells in this obscure place like the shrine
Of some great Saint, to which devotion
From severall parts brings daily men like pilgrimes.

DUKE of FLORENCE
Her name.

MONTALTO
Shee is wit, beauty, chastity, and all
That can make woman lovely to mans soule,
So farre from the capacitie of ill
That vertues in all other of her Sex
Like staines, but fit of her perfection:
And when is named all goodnesse in her titles,
The ornament, nay glory of them all
Is Domitilla Sir.

DUKE of FLORENCE
You speake her high,
And I may guesse by your description
My Lord, this Lady hath another name—
Shee is your mistresse.

MONTALTO
Not mine; she was created for some Prince,
And can beside her virtues, bring a fortune
Worth his embrace.

DUKE of FLORENCE
What charmes are in her lookes.

MONTALTO
Are you there Duke; this meeting was my project;
Things may succeede to my ambition,
If I doe noose your highnesse.

SIMPHOROSA
Please your Majestie.

KING of NAPLES
All things must please here.

DUKE of FLORENCE
I follow Sir.

SIMPHOROSA
This is a grace I ever must be proud of.

[Exeunt.

THE SECOND ACT

SCENE I

The Same.

BOMBO, IACAMO.

BOMBO
Have they almost dined? stay, stay a little:

IACAMO
The last course is o'th table;

Why doe not you waite?

BOMBO
That were a way indeede to be discovered!
No, the King shall pardon me; he has
Not seene me yet for all his cunning.

IACAMO
Whom doe you meane.

BOMBO
The King; thou art ignorant
Ile tell thee after dinner; 'ith meane time
Direct a wandring bottle of wine this way
And let me alone though I appeare not in't
I may have a humour to make a Maske if they
Stay supper.

IACAMO
Thou make a Maske!

BOMBO
I doe not say Ile write one, for I ha' not
My writing tongue, though I could once have read,
But I can give if neede be the designe,
Make worke among the Deale boards, and perhaps
Can teach 'em as good language as another
Of competent ignorance; things goe not now
By learning; I have read 'tis but to bring
Some pretty impossibillities, for Antemaskes
A little sence and wit dispos'd with thrift,
With here and there Monsters to make 'em laugh;
For the grand businesse to have Mercury
Or Venus Dandiprat to usher in
Some of the gods that are good fellowes dancing,
Or goddesses, and now and then a song
To fill a gap; a thousand crownes perhaps
For him that made it, and theres all the wit.

IACAMO
In what?

BOMBO
In getting of the money.

IACAMO
You are witty signior Bombo to advance
The muse, Ile fetch a bottle that you talk'd o',

BOMBO
If there be a superfluous Phesant
Twill quell my hunger for a time; I heare
Intelligence of an Oleo; if any
Such things may be recovered from the courtiers
That have keene appetites upon hunting dinners;
You shannot neede to enquire much after me.

[[Exit **IAMOCO** and re-enter **IACAMO** with a flask.

I shall be here abouts; why thou hast wings!

IACAMO
A bottle of rich wine.

BOMBO
Thou wert alwayes honest.

IACAMO
There's asking for my Ladies Secretary

BOMBO
I knew't; I am not here;
Doe they inquire already? come Ile pledge thee;
What wilt thou say if some body be sent for to Court.

IACAMO
Ile drinke some bodies health.

BOMBO
Th'art a good fellow, and this curtesie
Shall be remembred.

[Within call]
Iacamo!

IACAMO
I am cald.

BOMBO
Leave, leave your wicker, friend weele drinke a cup—

[Exit **IACOMO**.

When thou art gone; tis very excellent wine;
And now I have a stomacke like an edge toole;
But no good comes of idlenesse—tother cup;

The bottle growes light headed; how now friend?
No dish of meat appeare; nothing to shew
The Kitchin and the Wineseller are friends?
I would the Cooke were roasted!—honest Iacamo!

[Re-enter **IACOMO** with a dish of meat, and **PIETRO** with a flask.

I was thinking of a brace of Cocks just as you came.

IACAMO
I have retriv'd a covey of Partridge for thee.

PIETRO
And a cup of Greeke wine; Heeres to thee.

[Drinks.

BOMBO
I understand Greeke wine; Ile lose no time.

[Drinks.

IACAMO
What's this? a Booke?

BOMBO
No, tis my learned trencher.

[Lays the meat on the cover of the booke.

Which Schollers sometimes ease, Euclid they call it;
In my opinion this wing and legge
Is worth all bodies mathematicall;
Now let's dispute in Greek, to the Kings health.

[Drinks.

PIETRO
To me, Ile pledge.

[Drinks.

IACAMO
It shall goe round.

[Drinks.

BOMBO

And why doe you thinke my friend the King
Came hither with the Duke.

PIETRO
To dine.

BOMBO
Thy braines are in thy guts; you shall heare more;
Whats this?

IACAMO
Potato Bulley.

BOMBO
A cup of wine to cleare the passage; [Drinks] so;
Here is as they say Latine; here is Greeke, and
Here is for ought I know an Hebrew roote, most learnedly
Met together.

IACAMO
Heele be drunke presently.

BOMBO
Bottle in battle ray! present, give fire!

[Drinks.

So! as
You were; have they good stomacks Iacamo?
How feeds the King?

[Sets down the flask.

IACAMO
He was very pleasant with your Lady;
But the Duke feedes upon her lookes.

BOMBO
My Ladies health, my Lady little Domitilla's health.

PIETRO
Well said; about, about.

BOMBO
I am about another to our reverend Lady Simphorosa;

[Drinks.

So, so; this wine they say will make us see things double,
Here is but one Leg visible; well for this favour
Gentlemen if I be forced to live in court Ile make
You all in time; who can write or reade among you.

BOTH
None, none; we scorne it.

BOMBO
You shall have all preferment trust to me,
And marke my steps; heere to the curteous drinker;

[Drinks.

Now doe I finde a noble constitution in me, now
Could I leape; would thou wert any living Lady
In my way now.

IACAMO
Away; the Lords are risen.

BOMBO
The Lords doe rise and fall.

PIETRO
Hees paid; the King will come this way.

BOMBO
Every man goe his owne way; I wonnot see
The King for all this.

[Enter **GUIDO, ALOISIO, ALEXIO**.

Friend.

GUIDO
This is the Ladies Secretary, pray my Lords
Be acquainted with him.

BOMBO
Dee heare no body say he saw me, I wonnot
Be seene yet.

[He reeles in.

GUIDO
Though he be made a spectacle; but leave him
'Twas a handsome entertainement o' the sudden.

ALOISIO
A pretty hunting dinner; but did you not
Observe with what intention the Duke
Shot eyes on Domitilla.

ALEXIO
And the King
Applied all his discourse to her; I know not;
He has made no vow against a second marriage
But if he choose at home and looke at beauty.

GUIDO
Shees a very pretty talking Lady.

ALEXIO
Very ingenious.

ALOISIO
And with your favour, though she be no Court Lady.
Shee wants no confidence.

ALEXIO
What if the Duke be taken with her

GUIDO
Let him be taken a bed with her, tis my opinion
My Lord Montalto wonnot die for greefe ont.

ALOISIO
They are here.
Duke Montalto.

MONTALTO
Your grace is sad; excuse
My dilligence to waite on you; I could wish
If it made no intrusion on your thoughts,
I had opportunity to expresse
What might not be unworthy of your patience:

DUKE
To me?

[Enter **KING of FLORENCE**, leads **DOMITILLA**.

MONTALTO
The King.
This way Ladies to the Garden; let me have

The honour to attend you.

[Exit **DUKE of FLORENCE, MONTALTO**.

KING of NAPLES
Where's the Duke.

GUIDO
He tooke that way to the Garden Sir, with
The Lord Montalto.

KING of NAPLES
You may remove a little;

[Exit **GUIDO**.

You have no feare to trust your selfe with me.

DOMITILLA
I cannot Sir forget you are the King,
And in a Wildernesse could have no thought
With the least prejudice upon your vertue.

KING of NAPLES
You have the greater innocence at home
My intents are faire enough, and you may stand
The danger of a question; pray how old are you?

DOMITILLA
Although it be not held a welcome complement
To our Sex, my duty bids me not dispute;
I am fifteene my mother saies.

KING of NAPLES
And are
You not in love.

DOMITILLA
I must not charge my selfe
With so much ignorance to answer, that
I understand not what it meanes; I know
The word, but never could apply the sense,
Or finde it in a passion more then ordinary.

KING of NAPLES
Cupid hath lost his quiver then; he could not
Be armde, and let you scape, whose sole captivite
Would be more glory then the conquest made

As Poets faine upon the gods.

DOMITILLA
Tis language
With which you are pleas'd to mocke your humble handmaid.

KING of NAPLES
But this assures him blinde.

DOMITILLA
He would deserve
To lose his eyes indeede if he should aime
A shaft at me.

KING of NAPLES
Madam you have a heart.

DOMITILLA
To which no other
Flame can approach; then what shall light it to
Obedience of your will and my good mothers.

KING of NAPLES
Obedience to my will; what if it were
My will that you should love.

DOMITILLA
Sir, I doe love.

KING of NAPLES
Love with the warme affection of a mistresse
One Ile present a servant, why that blush;
The words are not immodest; there did want
No blood upon your cheeke to make it lovely;
Or does it slow in silence to expresse
That which your virgin Language would not be
So soone held guilty of, consent.

DOMITILLA
To what?

KING of NAPLES
To love by my direction a man
Whose worth considered shall deserve thee too,
And in the noblest way invite thy freedome
Untill the holy Priests declare, your hearts
Are knit into one blessing; theres no harme
In this.

DOMITILLA
Most royall Sir I know not, with
What words to say, you honour me; how can
One so unworthy as poore Domitilla
Be entertaind within your thoughts and care
In this high nature.

KING of NAPLES
Though your mother have
Made both her person and your selfe a stranger
To Court, I have had eyes upon your vertues
Which waited on by a most ample fortune,
I have studied to advance, if you'le accept
A husband of a my choise; what say you Madam?

DOMITILLA
I have a mother Sir.

KING of NAPLES
Shee shall thinke it fortunate
Bove expecation; you have not vowed your selfe
To a cold Nunnery.

DOMITILLA
Not I Sir.

KING of NAPLES
When
I shall declare how pretious he is
To my owne bosome.

DOMITILLA
Royall Sir, this language
Must needes prepare a welcome; I should thinke
My heart unlike another womans, not
To obey a charme so powerfull as your praise;
But when you are considered as my King,
Duty takes off the merit of my will
And humble every thought beneath obedience.

KING of NAPLES
His name is.

DOMITILLA
Pardon I beseech you Sir,
Conceale it yet; what gentle spirit walkes
Upon my blood; I dare not looke upon him

My hopes my feares; it is enough great Sir,
That you leave one within your thought, you would
Commend to Domitilla, one you love,
And pretious to your bosome; sure you blest him
With such a Character.

KING of NAPLES
It was too short.

DOMITILLA
My heart is a false Prophet [aside] tis a fate
Too good and great for Domitilla.

KING of NAPLES
Well his name shall be reserv'd; but when it opens
It selfe to your knowledge you will honour it,
And thanke me Domitilla; ith meane time
Let the opinion you have of me
Live in your trust, and make roome in your heart
To meete the husband I shall bring.

[Exit.

DOMITILLA
Why may not this be meant by his owne person?
More wonders have beene read in story; I
Finde thicke but amorous tremblings in my heart;
Hee's King; why not? love has done stranger things,
And can lead captive the proud heart of Kings.

[Exit.

SCENE II

The Same — A Garden

[Enter **DUKE of FLORENCE**, **MONTALTO**.

DUKE of FLORENCE
Here none can reach our voyce: be free and cleare.

MONTALTO
First let me kisse your hand, on which I sweare
To speake all truth; tis justice to your person,
Your merit and my faith; next though the secret
May both concerne and benefit your knowledge,

I shall desire your pardon

DUKE of FLORENCE
You prepare me
For wonder; if it be an act of Friendship
To me, it will become me to reward it,
Not thankes, nor pardon.

MONTALTO
But all truthes meet not
With charitable eares; there is a descant
That pleases not sometimes though the best art
Present it, if our sense be indispos'd
To patience and calme hearing.

DUKE of FLORENCE
Doe not doubt me.

MONTALTO
Twill not become me so much as in thought
To enquire how long, or with what firme devotion,
You affect the Princesse, Theodosia;
But Naples is more conscious, then to doubt
You bring a welcome treaty in your person,
And every voice and heart is busie with
The expectation of your marriage;
Whilst every eye bright with your stame is able
To light a Torch to Hymen; Virgins have
No other care then with what flowers sweet
As your owne name to adorne the smiling altars.

DUKE of FLORENCE
You promis'd Sir a secret.

MONTALTO
It will come
To fast upon your knowledge; have you never
Look'd from the prospect of your Pallace window,
When some faire sky courted your eye to reade
The beauties of a day, the glorious Sunne
Enriching so the bosome of the earth
That trees and flowers appear'd but like so much
Enamell upon gold; the wanton birds
And every creature but the drudging Ante
Despising providence, and at play and all
That world you measure with your eye, so gay
And proud, as winter were no more to shake
His Icy Lockes upon 'em, but the breath

Of gentle Zephire to perfume their growth,
And walke eternally upon the Springs;
When from a coast you see not, comes a cloud
Creeping as overladen with a storme
Darke as the wombe of night, and with her wings
Surprising all the glories you beheld;
Leaves not your frighted eyes a light to see
The ruines of that flattering day.

DUKE of FLORENCE
This Language
Carries both mystery and horror; pray
My Lord convey your meaning to my knowledge.

MONTALTO
I shall I had in vaine prepard you thus else;
Pardon againe the story; Theodosia,
More beautifull then the day I figur'd by her,
Is quite orecast and lookes through an Ecclipse
Upon your love: shee has no heart, but what
Another is possest of.

DUKE of FLORENCE
Ha!

MONTALTO
I know
It cannot but afflict your thoughts that all
Your expectation ripe and courted, to
The enjoying such a treasure as shee is,
Must finish in embracing of a shaddow,
Invited to a fable, not a bride
That should with joy dwell in your princely armes:
For Theodosia without sacriledge
Cannot be yours; shee is contracted.

DUKE of FLORENCE
How?
The King of Naples must not Sir ingage
Florence to such a mockery.

MONTALTO
Tis my duty
To cleare his honour in't he has a pure
Intention to make his sister yours; her close
Though honorable love's designd without
His knowledge, and you will but waste your rage
Vpon her destiny which will bury her

In her owne ruines, if your anger make
The King her enemie.

DUKE of FLORENCE
I doe not finde
My heart in any disposition
To breake at hearing of this newes, but wish it
Truth to prepare roomes for another guest;
The fairer Domitilla is here sainted [aside].

MONTALTO
Your excellencie—

DUKE of FLORENCE
Must not be thus affronted
Montalto, and returne with this dishonor.
Was there no cheaper person to be made
Ridiculous in Naples.

MONTALTO
Calme your blood,
I know you must resent it, but let not
Your passion make the world beleeve you should
Dispaire to finde one apter to your bosome;
The richest beauty in the world, your birth
And fortune must deserve and, and I should curse
My forward duty to your grace.

DUKE of FLORENCE
No more
I have considered better and although
Your love may merit thankes, yet this intelligence
Wonot concerne my faith; this cannot be Sir.

MONTALTO
My honour is ingaged then to convince you
Though with the hazard of my life and fortunes,
Both which must now depend upon your mercy;
Your breath shall make 'em bleed or live.

DUKE of FLORENCE
What meanes
Montalto?

MONTALTO
To translate the power of all
My Starres, and make you Lord of my whole fate
Theodosias heart Sir should be mine, by free

Gift of her selfe, who has beene pleas'd to take
My vowes in the exchange, which now may boast
Some time and growth, which could not be a sinne
Against your love, with which all that can spring
From me deserves no name, nor dare I take
Boldenesse to call her mine, who am a thing
Lighter then ayre in ballance with your grace
If you but chide the ambition, and could render,
Though I commit a rape on my owne life,
All that her love hath promis'd me.

DUKE of FLORENCE
Tis strange.

MONTALTO
But she let me take freedome to be plaine.

DUKE of FLORENCE
Is not to be reduc'd youle say.

MONTALTO
Sir, women
Love not with that safeguard upon their passion.

DUKE of FLORENCE
Shee has a wise art to dissemble then.

MONTALTO
Tis feare it should arive at the King knowledge.
In whose displeasure shee is lost and not
A will to mocke your grace, for whom there is
Another wound within her minde, that shee
Should weare a smiling summer in her brow
Yet frost within her heart, in which unhappily
Shee comes to neare the nature of the Adamant
Hard to your grace whom shee attracts; but love
Your wisedome knowes is in the volume of
Our fate decreede, whose periods when they are
By time made knowne; greatnesse on earth, that meanes
To play the tyrant with us, may have strength
To punish not reverse.

DUKE of FLORENCE
I am confirmde
And prosper in my thoughts [aside].

MONTALTO [aside]
It takes'

DUKE of FLORENCE
My Lord,
You have expression act of confidence
Which I must not betray though to my losse,
It is some happinesse to know this early;
We may be expected; you shall finde me Sir
A Prince, but no usurper.

MONTALTO
I am your creature
The King.

[Enter **KING of NAPLES, SIMPHOROSA, DOMITILLA, GUIDO, ALOISIO, ALEXIO.**

We build upon your piety
Untill some little time may call our loves
Out of this silence.

KING of NAPLES
You understand me Madam?

SIMPHOROSA
And am honor'd.

DUKE of FLORENCE [aside]
Her eyes beget new wonder; I shall be observ'd.

KING of NAPLES
Come, now to horse.

DUKE of FLORENCE
I shall attend; your entertainment has
Oblig'd us, Madam.

SIMPHOROSA
Twas not worth such guest;
But prayers and duty must supply.

KING of NAPLES
Now Madam you are a great part of my care
Depend upon me for a husband.

DOMITILLA [aside]
Ist not plaaine.

DUKE of FLORENCE
Madam another guest must take his leave,

That here would choose his pallace.

DOMITILLA
You are gratious, and but encourage more to honour you

MONTALTO
Ile creepe and kisse thy Altar love, allow
Them flame, and knit more charmes upon her brow.

[Exeunt.

THE THIRD ACT

SCENE I

Naples. A Part of the Palace.

DUKE of FLORENCE and **RIVIERO**.

DUKE of FLORENCE
Tis thy old quarrel gainst Montalto makes
Thee incredulous, I dare beleeve he loves
Theodosia.

RIVIERO
Tis not that I question Sir,
But that part which concernes her love to him
Sounds like a plot upon your nature, to
Secure his owne ambition.

DUKE of FLORENCE
Why the Princesse
May love; as great a heart has beene made stoope.

RIVIERO
Your grace should else in vaine court her your selfe
And late your highnesse thought shee meet your person
A faire designe of love, with all the soft
Behaviour of a Princesse.

DUKE of FLORENCE
But tis not
Impossible a Lady should dissemble.

RIVIERO
Allow her but the honour she was borne with,

And sheel'e not staine her blood so much.

DUKE of FLORENCE
But love
Must be obeyed, and prepossession
Of hearts is a lewd thing to wrastle with.
I make it my owne case, and if I lov'd
Another Lady better then the Princesse,
As every man's not proofe against all beauty,
I thinke I should be constant too; it would
Be something to remove me.

RIVIERO
Then the King?

DUKE of FLORENCE
He knowes not; & I have bound my selfe in honour
Not to betray, if they be decreed
To make a marriage; a soft destiny
Attend their loves.

RIVIERO
There is some mystery;
But will you rest and take for granted shee
Does love Montalto; if it be a truth
Y'are in the same condition when shee
Confirmes it.

DUKE of FLORENCE
Tis not good to be busie
In search of these unwelcome certainties;
There's hope while things are clouded in suspition.

RIVIERO
But so your jealousie may wound her honour,
Which you may cure by knowledge.

DUKE of FLORENCE
I will thinke on it;
Meane time let this dwell in that honest silence
You have possest; there is another secret
May follow.

RIVIERO
You must challenge my whole bosome,
And I am confident your highnesse will
Stere all your resolutions by honour,
Which in a Prince is sacred.

[Enter **SERVANT**.

SERVANT
Sir, the Lord
Montalto is comming up.

DUKE of FLORENCE
Then try your art upon him,
And informe your selfe, Ile take
My time to appeare.

[Exit **DUKE of FLORENCE**.

[Enter **MONTALTO**.

RIVIERO
I obey
My honour'd Lord.

MONTALTO
Most noble Philberto,
Where is the Duke?

RIVIERO
If youle but excuse a few minutes—

MONTALTO
Tis
My duty to attend.

RIVIERO
How is it with the Princesse my good Lord?

MONTALTO
The Princesse? shee is in health; why this to me?
Hee is of inward counsell with the Duke,
I must be resolute.

RIVIERO
I aske, because,
His grace intends a present visit to her,
And was but now in mention of your Lordship
To beare him company.

MONTALTO
I like not that;
He knowes he may command my services.

RIVIERO
He will deserve your love; pray my Lord tell me,
And let us be plaine breasted; you injoy
The King, as I, but with lesse stocke of merit,
The favour of his excellence; how affect you
The present state of things; wilt be a match?
There is loud expectation in the world,
And after all, my Master's fond to have it
Proceede; to these, I am of opinion
Theres no retreating now without dishonour;
Yet as I am Philiberto I much pittie
He should through any wound to your affection
Perfect his love.

MONTALTO
He has told you then the secret,
And not to waste more language, I collect
From what you have exprest, he does resolve
To destroy me; Montalto must be trod on.

RIVIERO
Not so my Lord.

MONTALTO
Yes, and my heart the ascent,
To his Hymeneall altar, which must be
Made crimson with the blood of a true lover.
His will be obey'd, Theodosia shall see
To advance her, Montalto will goe smiling
To his sacrifice, and after many prayers,
That shee may live the darling of his heart,
Ile change my acquaintance of this world to be
At peace in my owne ashes.

RIVIERO
You will not
Commit a violence upon your selfe?

MONTALTO
I sha' not neede; the thought of her will kill me
With as much silence as I goe to sleepe;
I onely shall bleed inward, and my life
Remove it selfe like a faire apparition
That vanishes to th'eye, and with lesse noise
Then a calme Summers evening; but when I
Am dead, tis not impossible, some may
Report Theodosia was but revish'd from me;

Feare of a brothers anger, and the tricke
Of polliticke states, that marry to knit power
Not hearts, did force her to Herares armes,
Whilst I, torne from the branch where I once grew,
Travell I know not whether in the aire.

RIVIERO
I begin
To thinke him worth some pitty.

MONTALTO
Into what
Vaine thing would the severe apprehension
Of greefe transforme us? coward, let the Duke
Move with all amorous haste to his delight,
And glory in the hope of his faire bride,
Mine by the gift of heaven, and hearts; but all
My flowers grow dully on their stalkes, and wither;
Let her gay Paranimphs with rosie Chaplets,
Which will take all their colour from her blush,
Attend on Theodosia to the Temple,
While as they goe, no rude winde shall be heard,
But so much breath of heaven as gently may
Lifting their loose haire up, whisper my wrong
To every Virgins care; let them be married,
Knit hands, and plight a ceremonious faith;
Let all the triumphs waste; let them be wasted,
And night it selfe brib'd with a thousand formes
Of mirth and Revells, till the night grow faint
And pale with watching,
Invite to bed; yet there he shall enjoy
But Theodosia's body, and not that
As his faire thoughts expect, perhaps the conquest
Of one whom he loved better.

[Exit **MONTALTO**.

[Enter **DUKE of FLORENCE**.

RIVIERO
How was that.

DUKE of FLORENCE
Now shall I trust him? if my sense mistake not
Theodosia may not be a Virgin.

RIVIERO
'Twas

His bold conclusion.

DUKE of FLORENCE
Where is now the honour
You talke of; durst Montalto charge her with
This staine, without his conscience to assure it.

RIVIERO
Yes, and to me this tenders him the more
To be suspected and I am so farre
From thinking shee affects Montalto, that
I am convinc'd he loves her not; can he
Have any noble thought of Theodosia,
That dares traduce her honour; thinke o' that;
And can revenge in any lover be
A reason to wound a Ladies fame; it tasts
Of ranke injustice, and some other end
Time will discover; and yet your grace is bound
To have his accusation confirm'd,
Or hant this spotted panther to his ruine,
Whose breath is onely sweete to poyson vertue.

DUKE of FLORENCE
What I resolve inquire not.

[Exit **DUKE of FLORENCE**.

RIVIERO
I see through
Mont altoes soule, and have beene so long tame
In my owne sufferings; but this will make
Him ripe for punishment; Andrugio and
My sonne!

[Enter **ANDRUGIO, OCTAVIO**.

OCTAVIO
I cannot with the wings of duty
Fly swift enough to prostrate my obedience
And welcome from a long supposed death,
My honourd father.

RIVIERO
Then I must appeare so.

ANDRUGIO
And let me give a sonne up to your blessing
Worthy your best prayers, and embrace; twas time

To bring you acquainted; he had else this night
Contriv'd Montaltoes tragedie at a Banquet,
For your revenge his active thoughts I could not
Counsell no longer patience.

RIVIERO
Thou hast but
Prevented me Octavio; I was
Weary of my concealement.

OCTAVIO
But my joyes are wilde,
And will I feare, transport me.

RIVIERO
My best friend,
And my owne spirited boy, feare not Montalto;
Hee's now upon a precipice; his fate
Stoopes with the glorious burden of his pride.
Things may be worth our counsell; we shall see
This prodigie that would be held a Starre,
And did so fright us with his streaming haire,
Drop like a Comet, and be lost i'th aire.

[Exeunt.

SCENE II

A Room in the Palace.

[Enter **MONTALTO**, **THEODOSIA**.

MONTALTO
Ist possible the day should be so old,
And not a visite from the Duke.

THEODOSIA
While he
Injoyes health, I shall easily forgive
A little ceremony.

MONTALTO
And a lover;
Your grace must chide him; other men may have
Excuse for their neglect of time, but he
That loves deserves no pardon.

THEODOSIA
Judge with charity
My Lord; the case may be your owne; you would
Thinke her a cruell mistresse, that should doome
Your life to exile, for not payment of
One ceremonious visite.

MONTALTO
Not where such
Perfection were to ingage my service Madam;
Pardon the bold comparison; death were not
Enough to punish that rude thought that could
Start from your bright Idea; or converse
With praters that did not first concerne your excellence;
I would not be ambitious of a blessing
But from reflex of yours.

THEODOSIA
You would expresse
A most officious servant to that Lady
Were honourd in your thought; but the Duke of Florence
And I shall make no such severe conditions.

MONTALTO
If he doe love you Madam, that will teach him
Above what ceremony prescribes to honour you.

THEODOSIA
If he doe love.

MONTALTO
Your graces pardon; I
Speake from an honest freedome taken from
The assurance of your goodnesse, that know better
How to distinguish truth; I am not judge
Of his breast Madam.

THEODOSIA
I suppose you are not.

MONTALTO
And yet being a man another way
Conclude his passions are but such as have
Beene read in humane nature.

THEODOSIA
What inferre you

From hence my Lord?

MONTALTO
Nothing but that a Prince
May be no Saint in love.

THEODOSIA
Howe's that?

MONTALTO
Twas in my feare I should displease.

THEODOSIA
Your will.

MONTALTO
Not for the Empire of the world; I shall
Repent I live with your suspition
Upon my humbl'd soule.

THEODOSIA
Pray Sir be free
Touching the Duke; I must know all; what ist
Makes him no Saint.

MONTALTO
Madam he is not dead,
And in his life I see no miracles.

THEODOSIA
You talk'd of love.

MONTALTO
No miracles of love;
He loves as other men that have profest
Devotion to a mistresse—but

THEODOSIA
What? speake
I charge thee by the memory of what
Thou dost affect most.

MONTALTO
Though it wound my selfe
Be arm'd and heare it; how I blush within me,
To tell your highnesse Florence has transplanted
His heart, and all his active thoughts are plac'd—

THEODOSIA
On whom?

MONTALTO
On Domitilla.

THEODOSIA
Ha.

MONTALTO
I did observe 'em Madam, at her mothers house,
Where we were lately feasted after hunting,
How strangely he was taken, how his eyes
Did wanton with her face, and on her haire
Tie many golden knots, to keepe love chalnde;
But these are but suspitions; he since
Confest to me in hope to winne me to
Negotiate his affaire, how at first sight
He tooke in desperate flames, and that shee rules
The intelligence of his soule; I heare the King
Hath sent for her to Court, which must give Madam
A dangerous opportunity to actuate
His ends with your dishonour; I was unwilling
To speake this knowledge of his hasty change,
But all my bonds of piety and faith
Would have beene forfeit into a long silence.

THEODOSIA
Shall I be thus affronted.

MONTALTO
We see Princes,
Whom we call gods on earth, in the affaires
Of love turne men agen.

THEODOSIA
For Domitilla.

MONTALTO
That's the dishonour Madam, and infects
My braine to thinke on't, and as much beneath
Your grace in all the ornaments of soule
And person as shee is in blood, if my
Impartiall thoughts may take so bold commission
To judge betweene your beauties.

THEODOSIA
Is it possible;

MONTALTO
Tis too certaine Madam; I should be
A villaine to accuse the Duke unjustly,
Or bring but shaddowes of a truth; for though
He be unworthy of your love that dares
Thus valew your perfections, below
That Phantom Domitilla, let not passion
Make you to rash in managing a cause,
On which depends your fame, compared to which
Ten thousand lives added to mine were nothing;
Observe him at next visit.

THEODOSIA
Ile study thankes Sir.

MONTALTO
You pay me with a blessing, if my name
But live within your memory.

THEODOSIA
This troubles me.

[Exit **MONTALTO**.

[Enter **KING of NAPLES** and **GUIDO**.

KING of NAPLES
Are they both come to court?

GUIDO
And in those lodgings were prepar'd.

KING of NAPLES
Tis well, and came they cheerefully?

GUIDO
Yes Sir, but something
I nigh discerne like trouble, and by starts
In Domitilla; but they are pleas'd with their
Remove, and waite all your commands.

KING of NAPLES
So leave us;

[Exit **GUIDO**.

Theodosia, whats the matter? art not well.

THEODOSIA
Where's the Duke.

KING of NAPLES
I thought to have met him here.

THEODOSIA
Is Domitilla come to Court?

KING of NAPLES
She is
By my command to waite on thee.

THEODOSIA
To rivall me.

[Exit.

KING of NAPLES
Howes that?
I meant her a wife for good Montalto,
As the reward of his just services;
He knowes it not, as he is ignorant
For whom I have prepar'd her; Rivall? strange
I must know more of this; shee is in nature
Too apprehensive; for although in love
Suspition to men a torment be,
There is no Fiend to womens jealousie.

[Exit.

SCENE III

Another Room in the Same.

Enter **DOMITILLA, BOMBO.**

BOMBO
You may doe what you will Madam; put me
Into fine clothes, and make an asse of me;
But should you wrap me in a Lyons skinne.

DOMITILLA
You have eares that will betray what beast you are.

BOMBO
Pray Madam tell me in six words of sence,
What shall I doe hete; Ile not see the King,
Though he have cunningly devis'd this tricke
Onely to bring me hither and betray me
To offices, make me at least an Idoll.

DOMITILLA
Whats that?

BOMBO
An Idoll in the Countrey I have read
A thing we call a worshipfull, a right worshipfull,
Descended from the house of the fac totums,
Lord of the soile, and Cocke of his owne dunghill.

DOMITILLA
You may be out of feare; you cannot reade now,
Nor set your name to a warrant.

BOMBO
All that nothing;
Ignorance every day comes into fashion,
And no meane statesmen now when they doe write
Their names, doe for their honours so conceive it,
You can hardly know a nobleman from a marke.

DOMITILLA
If you be an enemy to all preserment,
Your best way is to leave the world and turne
A lay Fryer.

BOMBO
No I finde no such thing in my constitution;
Every man is not bound to be Religious;
Men of my bulke and bearing should not fast so;
I am not given by nature to drinke water,
Or lye without a shirt; I have cornes Madam,
And I would make lesse conscience to undoe
My Shoomaker, then walke on wodden Pantables
I will indure to serve you still and dwell here,
So you conceale me from the King; tis not
That I doe owe his Majestie ill will;
I could indure him too upon condition,
He would make nothing on me.

DOMITILLA
Why he shall

Make nothing on thee take my word, or if
Thou hast a minde Ile pray him make thee lesse.

BOMBO
No, I would be a midling Christian;
But what will you doe here your selfe; youle be in.

DOMITILLA
With whom dost thinke.

BOMBO
And cast away your selfe
Vpon some pageant, one whose wit must be
Beholding to anothers Wooll to keepe it warme;
One that can dance and sing and wag his feather,
An artificiall Calfe carrier;
A youth that's sowed together by his Taylour,
And taken a peeces by his Surgeon.

DOMITILLA
Why how now Secretary.

BOMBO
I could say more.

DOMITILLA
Is this wit naturall?

BOMBO
You were best say
I got it here at Court; pray heaven I doe not
Loose what I brought; I had a holsome wit
I'th Countrey; aske the Parish and the Parson
For I kept company with those that reade
And learne wit now by the eare; if any slip from me,
As where there is a plenty some will out,
Here are so many wit catchers, a lost maidenhead
Is sooner found and set upon the shoulders
Of the right owner.

DOMITILLA
I preethe tell me Bombo,
And tell me truth, doe not you thinke your selfe
After all this a foole?

BOMBO
A foole; your servant Madam.

DOMITILLA
Ile speake thou maist be the Kings foole.

BOMBO
I thanke you,
I tell you Ile not see the King, or if I did,
Yes I looke like a foole, I could be angry,
But then you'd say I were a foole indeed.

DOMITILLA
Be not so passionate.

BOMBO
Wod I had beene a foole,
I would I had, for my owne sake I wish it,
I should not have beene tempted hither then,
By which I have indangered my good parts,
To State imployment; but Ile be wise enough,
He has not seene me yet nor shanot if
There be a witch in Naples, or a mist
That will be bought for money to walk the Court in
But take your course, and I were at home agen.

DOMITILLA
What then?

BOMBO
I would live in the Sellar, the Wine Sellar.

DOMITILLA
Tis your humility.

BOMBO
There were some fortification to be made
Against the Court invasions, countermines
Of sand and Sacke, a man might thrust himselfe
Among the bottles, and defie the world,
Be drunke, and not be cal'd out of his sleepe
To goe Embassadour.

[Enter **SIMPHOROSA**.

DOMITILLA
So, so, feare not,
Have a strong faith, and thou maist dye i' the countrey
For all this; here's my mother; let your care
Be now that none may interrupt us.

BOMBO
I will doe any thing but see the King.

[Exit

DOMITILLA
With pardon Madam you seeme full of thought.

SIMPHOROSA
I am studying Domitilla why the King
Should send for us to Court.

DOMITILLA
Mother you cannot
Mention the King in any act of his
That is not glorious and like himselfe;
He is the great example of a King,
But richer in his soule then state.

SIMPHOROSA
But why
To us this favour; to call us from those
Cold and obscure shades of a retirement
To plant us here neare his owne beames?

DOMITILLA
He has some meaning in't.

SIMPHOROSA
It tis yet darke to me.

DOMITILLA
We shall not staine his Court; his sister's but
A Lady of more distinction of birth;
Yet all that have beene Princes, came not to
Their state by a descent; the Heralds know
Some were not borne to purple and to scepters
That have beene Queenes; vertue has rais'd some,
And beauty has had many charmes to rule
The heart of Kings.

SIMPHOROSA
Whats all this Domitilla?
I hope you are not dreaming of a Queene;
Such wilde interpretation of the Kings
Favour to us cannot be made without
The forfeits of wits and duties which
Should teach us to containe our thoughts in their

Owne Spheare, and not to point them upon objects
Above our Levell.

DOMITILLA
I Betray my selfe,
When I sayd beauty had a power to charm
A King; it might acquit me from suspition
Of any hope to apply them so ambitiously;
Youle grant it just to love the King.

SIMPHOROSA
Our duties.

DOMITILLA
And he may where he please place his affection,

SIMPHOROSA
Leave that to her; it may concerne.

DOMITILLA
And shee
Thats mark'd for so great honour should be mad
To quarrell with her kinde fate.

SIMPHOROSA
What's all this
To thee?

DOMITILLA
To me; why mother ist not possible
A Lady not much fairer then my selfe
May be a Queene; great Princes have eyes
Like other men, and I should sinne against
What heaven and nature have bestowed on me,
Should my fate smile to thinke my face would be
The barre to such preferment.

SIMPHOROSA
Leaving this
Which is but mirth I know since we are falne
Into discourse of love, what would you answer
To Lord Montalto if he came a wooing
And recommended by the King?

DOMITILLA
I would
E'en recommend him to the King agen.

SIMPHOROSA
Is not his favorite worth your love, if he
Descend to be your servant.

DOMITILLA
As a servant,
He may be entertain'd, and were I Queene,
Perhaps he should be favorite to both;
And I would smile upon his services
In imitation of the King while he
Preserv'd his modest duty and his distance:

SIMPHOROSA
My daughter is transported, sure you are
No Queene sweet Domitilla.

DOMITILLA
Tis a truth,
Nor is Montolto yet my favorite.

SIMPHOROSA
I hope shee's not so miserable to affect
The King, by whose directions I prepare
Her for Montalto.

[Enter **BOMBO**.

BOMBO
A sprig of the Nobility cal'd Octavio
Desires accesse.

DOMITILLA
Admit him.

SIMPHOROSA
I must let this passion coole and leave her.

[Exit.

[Enter **OCTAVIO**.

OCTAVIO
Welcome to Court; why so; this sphere becomes you,
Or rather it takes ornament from you;
Now Domitilla shines indeede; your presence
Doth throw new beames about the Pallace Madam;
Before we look'd as we had lost our genius.

DOMITILLA
You came not from the King with any message,

OCTAVIO
I made this hast to tender my owne service.

DOMITILLA
You have no other suite to me?

OCTAVIO
Yes Madam.

DOMITILLA
Speake it.

OCTAVIO
And Ile not wander much about; shall I
Be admitted a young lover?

DOMITILLA
Men must not love till they be one & twenty,
They will be mad before they come to age else.

OCTAVIO
This Law was ne're decreed i'th Parliament
Of Cupid; such a Statute would undoe
Many sweet Virgins like your selfe; yet if
You'le promise to stay for me, I shall thinke it
A happy expectation; we are both
Young; we may choose each other Valentine
And couple, as we grow more ripe hereafter.

DOMITILLA
Ile aske you but one question my Lord,
What would you give to be the King of Naples?

OCTAVIO
I dare not thinke so ambitiously.

DOMITILLA
Tis modest: what if I cannot love under a Prince.

OCTAVIO
Can he be lesse, whom you will make happy
To boast in the possession of your faire
Person, a thousand provinces; those eyes
Are able to create another Indies;
All the delights that dwell in blessed Tempe

Divinely bud and blossome in your cheeke;
The treasure of Arabia's in your breath;
Nor Thebes alone, as to Amphions Lute
Stoopes to the heavenly magicke of your voyce,
But all the world.

DOMITILLA
No more of this; these praises
Are made for children, and will make truth blush;
They may fill up where nature is defective;
And were I Queene of Naples I should punish
Such flattery; but you are young and may
Outgrow this vanity.

OCTAVIO
You are mercifull.

DOMITILLA
I shall be ever so to you Octavio,
Let this incourage you to thinke I love you
In the first place, of those which are borne subjects;
If you will answer my respects forbeare
To question further.

OCTAVIO
I shall waite sometime, and kisse your hand.

DOMITILLA
And if my power may
Prevaile to doe you favour with the King,
Make your addresse.

OCTAVIO
Has not the court transform'd her.

[Exit.

DOMITILLA
Me thinkes I move upon a state already
And yet tis not the glory of his title
Affects my hope so much; his person's lovely,
And both together make the charme; I doe
Expect his royall presence; how shall I
Behave my lookes when he declares himselfe,

[Enter **IACAMO**.

IACAMO

Madam.

DOMITILLA
Admit not every Lord to trouble me;
I will take physicke; but Ile be observ'd;
You may frame some excuse to Ladies too
That presse their visite.

IACAMO
Tis the Duke.

DOMITILLA
The Duke?

IACAMO
Of Florence.

DOMITILLA
Princes must not be neglected;
That name gives him accesse; say I attend.

[Exit **IACOMO**.

[Enter **DUKE of FLORENCE**.

DUKE of FLORENCE
The acknowledgments I owe your favours Madam,
Late your rude guest brings me to kisse your hand.

DOMITILLA
Your excellence is pleas'd to interpret fairely
Of our intents.

DUKE of FLORENCE
And till occasion ripen
My whole discharge for your faire entertainment,
Madam, be pleas'd to weare these Diamonds,
Which of themselves betray their want of lusture,
And come with an ambition to recover
Flame from your smile.

DOMITILLA
It can be no dishonour
To take these from a Prince.
Enter Iacamo, whispers to Domitilla.
The King with wings,
Ile haste to meet him,

[Exit.

DUKE of FLORENCE
Gone, and so abruptly
Her businesse might allow her breath to thanke me
For my rich present; but Ile follow her;
I wo'd not meet the King here; if shee prove
Gentle, my heart I consecrate to love.

[Exit.

THE FOURTH ACT

SCENE I

A Room in the Palace.

Enter **KING of NAPLES** and **DOMITILLA**.

KING of NAPLES
My pretty Domitilla, now you are
My guest, tis fit whom I have made my charge
Should live within my eyes, welcome once more to Court.

DOMITILLA
You are bounty Sir it selfe, and binde
A Virgins prayers.

KING of NAPLES
What art thou yet prepar'd
To heare his name, I would declare thy husband.

[Enter **DUKE of FLORENCE**.

DUKE of FLORENCE
The King.

KING of NAPLES [aside]
The Duke; this confirmes it.

DUKE of FLORENCE
Unlucky fate he has spied me.

KING of NAPLES
Thou shalt have
A little patience, while the Duke and I

Change some discourse in private.

DOMITILLA
I Obey

[Exit.

DUKE of FLORENCE
He is sent off; I hope the King is not
In love with her himselfe.

KING of NAPLES
Now my Lord, what
Alone, I see you can addresse your selfe
To a handsome Lady.

DUKE of FLORENCE
He has prevented mē.
Where I receive favour I shall never
Want heart to acknowledge.

KING of NAPLES
That rule binds to all.

DUKE of FLORENCE
It does but with distinction, to pay.

KING of NAPLES
But with distinction to pay,
First love to those that best deserves it from us.

DUKE of FLORENCE
Tis justice Sir.

KING of NAPLES
This granted, there's another
Whom though you can forget, my sister Sir
Deserves to be remembred.

DUKE of FLORENCE
You are jealous
That I visite this Lady.

KING of NAPLES
That were onely
To doubt; I must be plaine; Florence has not
Beene kind to Naples to reward us with
Affront for love, and Theodosia must not

Be any Princes mockery.

DUKE of FLORENCE
I can
Take boldnesse too, and tell you Sir it were
More for hēr honour, shee would mock no Prince
I am not lost to Florence yet, though I
Be Naples guest, and I must tell him here
I came to meet with faire and Princely treaties
Of love, not to be made the tale of Italy,
The ground of Scurrile pasquills, or the mirth
Of any Lady, who shall preingage
Her heart to anothers bosome, and then sneake
Off like a tame despised property,
When her ends are advanc'd.

KING of NAPLES
I understand not
This passion; yet it points upon something
That may be dangerous to conclude; Theodosia
Is Naples sister, and I must not see
Her lost to honour, though my kingdome bleed
To rescue her.

DUKE of FLORENCE
Now you are passionate;
Tis I must be repair'd; my name is wounded,
And my affection betrayed; your sister
That lookes like a faire starre, within loves skie
Is falne, and by the scattering of her fires
Declares shee has alliance with the earth,
Not heavenly nature.

KING of NAPLES
Are my senses perfect;
Be clearer Sir; teach me to understand
This prodigie; you doe not scorne our sister?

DUKE of FLORENCE
Not I; as she has title to your blood
Shee merits all ambition, shee is a Princesse,
Yet no staine to her invention, we are paralells
Equall, but never made to meet.

KING of NAPLES
How's this?

DUKE of FLORENCE

Truth is my witnesse I did mean to bring
No ceremonious love, untill I found
Her heart was given from me, though your power
Contract our bodies.

KING of NAPLES
Stay and be advis'd,
And if your doubts by some malitious tongue
Framed to abuse my sister, and your selfe,
Have rais'd this muteny in your thoughts, I have
A power to cure all.

DUKE of FLORENCE
Sir you cannot.

KING of NAPLES
Not to court thee for her husband, wert possest
Of all, ore which our Eagle shakes his wings,
But to set right her honour; and ere I challenge
Thee by thy birth, by all thy hopes and right
To fame, to tell me what seditious breath
Has poyson'd her; heare what my sister sends
By me so late, time is not old in minuts,
The word's yet warme with her owne breath; pray tell
The Duke saies she, although I know not from
What roote his discontents grow, to devote him
To Domitilla.

DUKE of FLORENCE
How does shee know that?

KING of NAPLES
Whose beauty has more spell upon his fancy,
I did contract my heart, when I thought his
Had beene no stronger to his tongue, and can
Not finde within it since, what should divert
His princely thoughts from my first innocence;
Yet such is my sterne fate I must still love him;
And though he frame his heart to unkinde distance,
It hath imbracing vertue upon mine,
And with his owne remove, drawes my soule after him;
If he forget I am a Princesse, pray
Let Naples doe so too; for my revenge
Shall be in prayers, that he may finde my wrong
But teach him soft repentance, and more faith.

DUKE of FLORENCE
All this must not betray my freedome Sir.

KING of NAPLES
Youle not accuse our sister of dishonour.

DUKE of FLORENCE
I would not grieve you Sir to heare what I
Could say; and presse me not for your owne peace;
Fames must be gently toucht.

KING of NAPLES
As thou art Florence speake.

DUKE of FLORENCE
I Shall displease;
Yet I but tell her brother that doth presse me;
Lucrece was chast after the rape; but where
The blood consents, there needs no ravisher.

[Exit.

KING of NAPLES
I doe grow faint with wonder there's enough
To blast an apprehension, and shoote
A quaking through the valiant soule of man;
My sisters blood accus'd, and her faire name
Late chast as trembling snow, whose fleeces clothe
Our Alpine hills, sweet as the Roses spirit
Or Violets cheeke, on which the morning leaves
A teare at parting, now begins to wither,
As it would haste to death, and be forgotten;
This Florence is a Prince that does accuse her;
And such men give not faith to every murmur
Or slight intelligence that wounds a Lady
In her deare honour; but shee is my sister;
Thinke of that too; credit not all, but aske
Of thy owne veines what guilty flowings there
May tempt thee to beleeve this accusation.

[Enter **THEODOSIA**.

'Tis shee;
Th'art come Theodosia to my wishes.

THEODOSIA
What does distract you Sir.

KING of NAPLES
I have done your message to the Duke, and finde

He does love Domitilla.

THEODOSIA
Her he shall meete and marry in Elisium.

KING of NAPLES
What meane you?

THEODOSIA
I have shooke off my tamenesse; doe not hinder
My just revenge; Ile turne their triumphs into death.

KING of NAPLES
There is a question of more consequence
Thou must resolve; it does concerne thee more
Then thy owne life.

THEODOSIA
You fright me.

KING of NAPLES
Are you honest?

THEODOSIA
Honest.

KING of NAPLES
I could have us'd the name of chaste,
Or virgin; but they carry the same sence;
Put off thy wonder Theodosia,
And answer me by both our parents ashes,
Which now are frighted in the urne, and scarse
Contain'd beneath their marble, while their same
Bleeds in my wounded honour art thou still
My sister without staine; upon thy chastity
Tell me and answer truth, for both our lives.
Nay, nay, there is no time for thy amaze;
Hast thou not lost thy selfe and beene injoyed;
I blush to name the way.

THEODOSIA
Never.

KING of NAPLES
Agen.

THEODOSIA
By all the good we hope for I an innocent

As your owne wishes.

KING of NAPLES
Th'art my vertuous sister.

THEODOSIA
But by your love and all that bound to
Be just, now let me know my strange accuser.

KING of NAPLES
Thou shalt know that hereafter; let thy thoughts
Live in their owne peace, and dispute not mine.

[Exit.

[Enter **DOMITILLA**.

DOMITILLA
Not speake to me; he fround too; sure I have not
Displeasd him; wherefore stayes the Princesse?

THEODOSIA
Shew spirit now or never. Domitilla
The greatest part of my affliction;
Let my revenge begin here [aside].

DOMITILLA
Your grace does honour your unworthy servants;
And if I might beseech one favour more,
Tis but to know what has displeas'd the King.

THEODOSIA
Must you be of counsell with his passions;
What hath advanc'd you to this boldnesse?

DOMITILLA
Pardon,
Why does your grace put on those angry lookes;
I never did offend you in a thought.

THEODOSIA
Cunning dissembler, yes, and tis thy death
Must satisfie; yet ere I give thee punishment
Tell me what impudence advanc'd thy thoughts
So high in our dishonour was where none
In your owne for me of blood fit for your love,
But you must flatter your prou? hopes with one
So much above thy birth? Though he in frailty

Consent to make thee great, dar'st thou accept it,
And with my shame aspite to be his equall;
Disclaime these hopes, and sweare never to love him.

DOMITILLA
Madam.

THEODOSIA
Doe, or with this I will secure my feares,
And stand the malice of all other fate.

DOMITILLA
Heare me.

THEODOSIA
Be briefe.

DOMITILLA
I know not by what genius prompted Madam,
To live or die, more happily, I have no
Feare of your rage, which is so farre from making
Me sinne against my love, it has inlarg'd
My heart, which trembles not to be loves martyr;
I can forgive your hand too, if you promise
To tell the King how willing I die for him.

THEODOSIA
The King; thou lov'st the Duke.

DOMITILLA
Hee's not concern'd
In my affection; I have no thought
Of any Prince alive, but your owne brother;
Such an example of loves folly have
My starres decreed me; yet if pride and duty
May in one action meete and be good friends,
Both shall assist my last breath which shall offer
Humbly the King, and his affaires to heaven
This he will pardon, shall he know it done
By me more sit to die then live for him.

THEODOSIA
Alas poore Domitilla; shee is wounded
As deepe as I; rise and forgive my jealousie;
I cannot promise thee to be my sister,
But I will love thee like one; let us call
A counsell of our thoughts, and mingle sorrowes;
Yet when we have done all, and tyr'd our breath,

There is no cure for love, but love or death.

[Exeunt.

[Enter **KING of NAPLES** and **MONTALTO**.

KING of NAPLES
How will Montalto counsell me; I am
Wilde with the repetition.

MONTALTO
The Duke
Lay such a blacke aspersion on your sister;
Tis blasphemy to honour; but as soone
He may pollute the Sunne beames, or defile
The dew of heaven ere it approach the earth
Make us beleeve the rockes of ice doe flame,
And may indanger the north starre; my wonder
Will make me reasonlesse; it throwes a poyson
On your whole family, a staine so deepe
And so prodigious, all the blood within
His Dukedome wo'not purge it; could he finde
No excuse for his revolt to Domitilla,
But blasting the sweet Princesse.

KING of NAPLES
Domitilla
Whom I must tell you I already have
Prepar'd to be thy bride, as an addition
To the reward I owe thy services.

MONTALTO
Prepard for me? you are too bountifull
In you I kneele both to my king and father;
But my aspiring will be satisfied
To be your servant still: in your grace I
Injoy the bride my heart affects; let me
Grow old with duties here, and not translate
My affection till my weary soule throw off
The burden of my dust.

KING of NAPLES
No more: in this
One act, Ile build a monument of my love
To thee, and my revenge upon the Duke;
Thou instantly shalt marry Domitilla;
Her Beauty, Blood and Fortune will deserve thee.

MONTALTO
I am your creature; but how this may inflame
The Duke.

KING of NAPLES
Tis meant so.

MONTALTO
But your sisters fame
Were worth your first care; this may be done
With more accesse of joy when shee is righted:
You have beene pleasd to heare my counsell Sir
And not repented.

KING of NAPLES
What would'st thou advise me?

MONTALTO
The Duke is young and apt to erre; you cannot
Preserve your hospitable Lawes to affront
Him openly, nor will it be thought prudence
To let loose these suspitions to the descant
Of peoples tongues; th'aire is dangerous;
Let me search the Dukes bosome, for the spring
Of this dishonour.

KING of NAPLES
How?

MONTALTO
Mistake me not;
Philoberto is his secret consellour,
And the receiver of his thoughts; leave me
To manage this great worke; I have a way
To every angle of his heart; meane time
Be pleas'd to keepe your person but retired;
A silent discontent will fright him more,
And arme us with full knowledge.

KING of NAPLES
Wise Montalto,
I like thy honest counsell, and obey it;
But lose no time.

[Exit.

MONTALTO
It never was more pretious;

My essence is concern'd and every minute
Brings a fresh seige against Montaltoes life;
There's none but Philoberto conscious
To my last accusation of the Princesse;
Then hee must be remov'd; delayes are fatall;
Ile poyson him to night; I have the way;
This done, the Duke may follow, or be brib'd
With Domitillaes person to quit Naples.

[Enter **GUIDO**, **ALOISIO**, **ALEXIO**.

GUIDO
My honour'd Lord.

MONTALTO
Guido, Aloisio;
Why make I this distinction y'are but one,
To your Montalto, have one heart and faith;
Your love and dilligence must now be active.

GUIDO
You have deserv'd us.

ALEXIO
Lord of our fortunes.

GUIDO
Wee are your creatures,
Bound by all Law and conscience of the court
To serve your ends.

MONTALTO
Tis but to waite close
And contrive excuses, if the Duke
Desire accesse to the King.

GUIDO
This all.

MONTALTO
Be carefull
None of his traine nor faction be admitted,
In speciall Philoberto; if he appeare,
Present my service, and desire to speake with him;
This is no mighty Province gentlemen
To waste you much; yet this neglected will
Destroy my tall fate, in whote fall you must
Stoope and be strucken dead with the large ruines.

GUIDO
Kill us not first by your suspition;
We looke upon you as out destimy;
Prosper as we are faithfull.

MONTALTO
You divide me.

ALEXIO
There is much trouble in his face, how e'er
Let us be firme; is not this Philoberto?

[Enter **RIVIERO**.

RIVIERO
My honor'd Lords.

GUIDO
We are proud to be your servants.
RIVIERO
I am yours; where is the Lord Montalto.

ALOISIO
New gone from us, and desires to speake with you,
And is gone either to your lodging or the Dukes.

RIVIERO
I have some affaires with the King, and that
Dispatch'd Ile waite upon him.

GUIDO
We are confident
You will excuse us; we receiv'd command
That none should interrupt him.

RIVIERO
I come from the Duke.

ALOISIO
His excellenct will conster it our duties.

RIVIERO
This was not wone.

ALOISIO
We dare not sit dispute
Our masters pleasure.

GUIDO
Perhaps his confessor is with him.

RIVIERO
Perhaps there is some cunning; nay preserre
The businesse of the soule, I may presume
He has no long Catalogue to account for.

GUIDO
You have not beene of counsel with his conscience;
We doe not use to limit his devotions.

RIVIERO
Tis pious, and you three by, by computation
Montaltoes knaves here plac'd, to keepe away
Discoveries: in spight of all your subtilties,
The king shall know my minde, and understand
The history of your patrons and your service;
Let time speak your reward in your owne chronicles.

ALOISIO
You not forget my Lord Montalto has
Desire to speake with him.

RIVIERO
Tis all my businesse;
Be carefull of your watch and looke about you,
Some Wee sell may get in else.

GUIDO
Does he jeere us?

ALEXIO
Let him; his Embassy is not perform'd.

[Enter **DUKE of FLORENCE, MONTALTO**.

MONTALTO
You doe amaze my understanding Sir
To require I should justifie a tale
Made to the blemish of so chaste a Lady.

DUKE of FLORENCE
Did not your Lordship tell such a story
To Philoberto in my lodgings.

MONTALTO

I date his molice, to affront; and tis not
Done like your selfe to sully with one breath
Two sames.

DUKE of FLORENCE
Shall I not credit my owne eares?

MONTALTO
Deare Sir, collect your selfe, and let not passion
To Domitilla whom you may passesse,
Here after make you so unjust.

DUKE of FLORENCE
Deare Machiavill
This will not doe; the King shall know your stratagems.

MONTALTO
Goe threaten babes; this would exalt my rage,
But I remember you're a guest to Naples:
Nor would I grieve the genius of my country,
To place my owne revenge above her honour.

DUKE of FLORENCE
Poore shaddow.

MONTALTO
Now.

[Drawes a dagger at the **DUKE'S** back.

'T will not be safe; you know your change [aside to **GUIDO**].

[Exit.

GUIDO
We are proud to see your excellence in health.

DUKE of FLORENCE
Where is the King?

ALOISIO
A little busy, Sir.

ALEXIO
Not yet I thinke, he is at his prayers.

DUKE of FLORENCE
Ile adde to his Letanie.

GUIDO
It wo'not neede;
I thinke his ghostly father can direct him,
With whom he is in private.

DUKE of FLORENCE
I know not
How to interpret this; I want Philoberto.

[Exit.

[Enter **OCTAVIO**.

OCTAVIO
Your graces
Servant; he lookes displeas'd.

GUIDO
My Lord Octavio.

OCTAVIO
Your servant Lords.

GUIDO
You meet the Duke.

OCTAVIO
His face shewed discontent.

ALOISIO
We summe our fortunes in Montaltoes smile,
By whose commands we have denyed the Duke
Accesse to'th King.

OCTAVIO
You have done well; it much
Concernes my Lord; his and all our fate
Depends upon't; continue still your care
And circumspection, and while I am within
Let none be admitted.

[Exit.

GUIDO
Let us alone;
A spirit may have the device to enter,
But if he have so much body as a Gnat

Ile know his errand; whoes this; oh it tis
My Lady Domitillaes Secretary.

[Enter **BOMBO**, gayly dressed.

BOMBO
Here are so many trickes, and turnes, and dores
I'these Court lodgings, I have lost my selfe.

GUIDO
Master Secretary.

BOMBO
Twas you betrayd me to the King, and caus'd
My Ladies to be sent for, with more cunning
To bring me hither; but alls one, he has
Not seene me yet not sha'not; which
Is my way out of this labyrinth.

ALOISIO
Why are you so unwilling the King should see you?

GUIDO
Or to live in Court; me thinkes this habite
Becomes you now; does it not my Lord.

ALEXIO
He lookes like a true Hero.

BOMBO
You are beside the story Sir; I did reade once
That Hero had no upper lip; shee was
A Lady of Leanders lake.

GUIDO
A wit? theres a new word; now for the Hellespont,
Heele make a subtile courtier.

BOMBO
It has undone me.

ALOISIO
Vndone thee how?

BOMBO
I know not whether it be my wit or clothes,
Or disposition of the place, or all
Together, but I am sure I am in love,

I finde it by the losing of my stomacke;
I am most strangely in love.

GUIDO
With whom?

BOMBO
I know not.

ALOISIO
Can you not guesse.

BOMBO
I hope tis with my selfe, for I did vow
When my first mistresse dyed which was,

GUIDO
What?

BOMBO
A dairy maide that we had i'th Countrey,
To love no living woman bove an houre;
Shee was the very creame of all her Sex;
Oft have we churn'd together.

GUIDO
And drunke healths
In Butter-milke.

ALOISIO
But doe you hope you are in love with your selfe Sir.

BOMBO
Marry doe I Sir; is that so wonderfull at Court?

GUIDO
You are pleasant.

ALOISIO
Lets be rid on him.

GUIDO
Come you shall now speake with the King,
And he shall knight thee; more honours may follow.

BOMBO
You shall excuse me; put your honours
Upon some body else.

GUIDO
Doe you know what tis?

BOMBO
I have not read of late.

ALOISIO
But you are much given to hearing,
What is honour.

BOMBO
Honour a buble is that is soone broke,
A Gloworme seeming fire, but has no smoake.

ALOISIO
There's fire and water.

BOMBO
And smoake for ayre;
A painted Sun-beame, peece of gilded Chaffe,
And he that trusts leanes to a broken staffe.

GUIDO
You should have reconcil'd the foure elements
To the conceit; there was fire, aire, water;
Wheres the earth.

BOMBO
Oh he that leanes to a broken staffe shall
Finde that presently.

[Enter **KING of NAPLES** reading a paper, **OCTAVIO**.

GUIDO
The King.

BOMBO
King bee your leave; I vanish.

[Exit **BOMBO**.

KING of NAPLES
This paper contains wonder; tis not possible.

OCTAVIO
Upon my lise Sir, Philoberto can demonstate these.

KING of NAPLES
The Divell has not art
To abuse us so; this will require some counsell;

[Enter **MONTALTO**.

Hee's here,

MONTALTO
Leave us.

[Exeunt **LORDS**.

MONTALTO
Sir your pleasure.

KING of NAPLES
Is all in thee; hast met with Philoberto?

MONTALTO
Not yet.

KING of NAPLES
No matter; I have thought upon't,
And doe conclude it best to let things passe
Yet in a dreame; choise and enquiry may
Awake suspition upon innocence.

MONTALTO
You cannot thinke her guilty Sir.

KING of NAPLES
I am not
Without some feares; I have collected things
Since we conferr'd, that stagger my good thoughts.

MONTALTO
Of her you cannot; Sir unthinke agen,
What ever would betray her to your jealousy;
A Virgins Monument cannot be more chaste
Ith Temple.

KING of NAPLES
Yes, yes; we may be all cozend;
And therefore let her passe among things desperate;
Yet were I certaine shee were spotted thus,
As tis but a young Leprosie upon her,
I could wish heartily my Sister timely

Married, not to the Duke that would betray us,
But to some one I know not, who could love
Vs both, so well as be that rare friend
And save our honours.

MONTALTO
Doe you then suspect her.

KING of NAPLES
Oh the Dukes Character had a powerfull sence;
And who knowes but shee may be lost by one
Not fit to make her reparation;
Could any Nobleman be found in Naples
To binde her wound up by so great an act
Of secrecy and marriage; but some winde
May listen and convey, I know not whether,
What my sad breath has scatter'd in the aire;
Thy Master has no servant that dares take
One sorrow from him.

MONTALTO
You are Sir provided
Of more then that can rise to in my service.

KING of NAPLES
Canst thou be so compassionate to lose
Thy hopes of richer beauty, for my sake?
Darst thou with all this knowledge hide her stain,
And marry her?

MONTALTO
My duty to your Majestie
Shall marry me to death; let not this trouble
The quiet of your heart; Ile take Theodosia,
And thinke upon her as shee had the whitenesse
Of my good Angell.

KING of NAPLES
Th'art a miracle;
Teach me but which way I may reward this love;
Till now I had no poverty; thy worth
Will make me everlastingly in debt;
What shall I say?

MONTALTO
Great Sir, no more; your favours
Flow from a bounty, which hath onely heaven
Above it.

KING of NAPLES
They are all trifles; let me see,
Is nothing in thy power to make thee finde
My gratitude? how barren are we, wealth,
Honour.

MONTALTO
Ther's nothing good or great you have not
Freely possest me with; your favours would,
So mighty have they falne upon me, rather
Expresse a storme, and I had sunke beneath
The welcome violence, had not your love
From whence they flowed, inabled me to strength
And manly bearing.

KING of NAPLES
I was inprovident
To reserve nothing, or it was a fault
In thee to be so prodigall of merit
In thy past services; canst thou thinke of nothing
Worth my addition.

MONTALTO
Nothing Sir.

KING of NAPLES
I have it,
And thanke my better genim I have it,
Such a reward Montalto that I dare
Be modest yet pronounce, never did Prince
Exceede it to his friend.

MONTALTO
Sir you amaze me,
And shame my want of merit.

KING of NAPLES
In the title,
Let Kings peruse the benefit and study
An imitation to their best loved creatures;
Th'are great as fortune can invent; Ile teach thee
A way Montalto, to know all thy friends.
And enemies.

MONTALTO
That were a pretious knowledge,
Were it in nature; with your highnesse pardon

The hearts of men are not to be measured
With what we reach the starres, or fathome Seas;
Oh he thats active in a state has more.
Chainde to him by the power and strength of office,
Then genuine respect; and tis not worth
Or person, but the fortunes of a Statesman
That sometimes men adore.

KING of NAPLES
Tis true; and therefore
I am proud in this that I can teach thee looke
Into mens soules, to know 'em fit for scorne, or
Thy embraces.

MONTALTO
How may this Sir be done?

KING of NAPLES
Almost 'ith twinckling of an eye too.

MONTALTO
Strange.

KING of NAPLES
I seeme to frowne upon thee.

MONTALTO
How Sir?

KING of NAPLES
Doest apprehend me; I will counterfeit
That I am displeas'd with thee; doe not mistake me,
And have it voic'd about the Court, thou art
Consin'd, doest marke; at this will all thy enemies
Whose hearts thou canst not see, their tongues before
By thy great power silenced, joyne in faction
Complaine, discover their whole stocke of malice,
Tickling their spleenes, that thou art out of favour,
Whom I shall heare and smile at; then all those
Whose honest soules deserve thee, will rise up,
The champions of thy same o'th other side
And be so many Oratours to make
Thy faith and honour shine; when this done,
The scene is chang'd, I send for thee; thou commest
With a most glorious traine; and then Ile smile,
Take thee agen i'th sight of all, discover
Twas but a tricke, thy friends keepe still thy bosome,
And thou in triumph shoot'st a scorne with mine

To strike all envie dumbe; Ist not a rate one?
I cannot doe enough for thee Montalto.

MONTALTO
You have found out a way I must confesse;
But with your pardon, I shall be more able
To do: you service in the other ignorance,
Then run a desperate hazard in this knowledge;
Some hold it sinne, and capitall enough
To have the Princess favour, which once lost
Though but in suspition; they may rage,
And like a torrent rise to o'rewhelme nature.

KING of NAPLES
These sha'not wound thee.

MONTALTO
And how other Indges
May wrest the actions of a man imployed
Though ne're so faithfull to his King and state.

KING of NAPLES
I am confident of thy justice and decree,
Thy triumph in't; thy goodnesse thus conspicuous
Renders thee loved, and fit for Theodosia
When she is brightest; the Sunne never smiled
More cherefull upon teeming earth,
Then I to finde thee perfect; for I doe
But seeme displeas'd; come, I will have it so;
If thou dost love me, no dispute, but let me
Pursue my fancie meant to doe thee honour.
Who waites?

[Enter **LORDS**.

Now it begins;
Attend my Lord Montalto to his Chamber,
Where our will is, he be consin'de untill
Our pleasure further knowne.

GUIDO
How's this?

ALEXIO, ALOISIO
Confin'd!

KING of NAPLES
No ceremony Sir; when that's done,

We ease you of the trouble too of waiting;
You know the way my Lords to your owne lodgings,
From whence on perill of our anger stirre not
Vntill wee send for you—Octavio.

GUIDO
Doe we not dreame.

MONTALTO
Something wo'd creepe
Like a dead sleepe upon me; I am in
A Labirinth; but hence with coward feare;
I know the worst; grim death can but translate
Me hence, and there's an end of death and fate.

[Exeunt.

THE FIFTH ACT

SCENE I

Naples – A Room in the Palace.

SIMPHOROSA, THEODOSIA, DOMITILLA.

THEODOSIA
He conforted and counsel'd Domitilla;
I have my part in loves affliction.

SIMPHOROSA
This I fear'd

[Enter **IACAMO**.

I must acquaint the King; where is your fellow
Bombo? his mirth might now be seasonable.

IACAMO
Hee's gone Madam.

SIMPHOROSA
Gone, whither?

IACAMO
Backe to the country house; he heard of my Lord
Montaltoes disgrace, and the feare of his supp'ying

The place of a favorite, sent him away this morning
With all his moveables; the countrey he saies
Is wholesome, where he will dye without feare or wit when
His time comes; he durst not stay to see the King.

[Exit **IACAMO**

SIMPHOROSA
Would we had still beene strangers to the Court;
Leave us; my daughter is much bound to your grace.

DOMITILLA
It is the King you speake of; pray be carefull
You speake all goodnesse of him, he deserves it,
And will when I am dead.

SIMPHOROSA
Ile lose no time.

[Exit.

THEODOSIA
I wish it prosper.

DOMITILLA
I dare not say the King dissembles with me;
That were a fault beyond my love; but sure
Something he said that made my heart beleeve
He did not meane me for another; and
Montalto, whose reward I must be thought,
Is now consin'd, and under his displeasure.

THEODOSIA
He will have more care of his honour then
To place thee so unworthily; Montalto
Has plaid the cunning traytour with our loves,
If I may trust thee noble Philoberto
That told me the whole story of his falsehood,
Which I before suspected.

DOMITILLA
And if he should dispise me as tis justice,
Will heaven be angry if I love him still;
Or will the King call it a treason in me?
If hee doe, I can willingly dye for't,
And with may last words pray he may live happy;
But why am I this trouble to your grace?
My story is not worth one of your minuts;

Deare Madam pardon me, and teach me how
To make my time more happy, spent in something
That may concerne your highnesse; you doe love too.

[Enter **IACAMO**.

IACAMO
Madam, the Duke of Florence.

THEODOSIA
How the Duke?

DOMITILLA
Why does he visite me? Madam indeed
You may beleeve I love him not.

THEODOSIA
Admit him
I preethe, and conceale me Domitilla;
I know he comes a wooing to thy beauty;
I preethe let me heare the second part.

[Exit.

DOMITILLA
I shall against my owne desires obey you.

[Enter **DUKE of FLORENCE**.

DUKE of FLORENCE
The ambition of my eyes can not be thought
Immodest, if they ever wish to dwell here;
They have found their light agen; let no misfortune
Be a second cause to bury me in darkenesse.

DOMITILLA
Your graces pardon, if my haste to attend
The King and his commands made me appeare
Rude when I left your excellence.

DUKE of FLORENCE
This does more
Then satisfie.

DOMITILLA
I know not how I may
Stand guilty in your thoughts by keeping a
Rich Caskanet.

DUKE of FLORENCE
You honor'd me to accept it.

DOMITILLA
But with a blush I must remember too
I did not thanke you; there was want of time
Or manners; I must leave it to your mercy,
And would by any duty to your grace
Expiate my errour.

DUKE of FLORENCE
Madam it is not worth
The mention of this gratitude; Your breath
Makes the oblation rich, and me who am
Encourag'd by your virtue, to present you
With something of more valew, then a world
Of these poore empty glories; I dare give you
My heart Madam.

DOMITILLA
Blesse your grace from such a meaning.

DUKE of FLORENCE
Can you be cruell to it?

DOMITILLA
I ne're had
The confidence to looke upon a wound;
And such a bleeding object as your heart
Would fright my senses.

DUKE of FLORENCE
You are more ingenious
Then not to understand that I meane love;
I love you Madam, best of all your sex.

DOMITILLA
You cannot Sir, you dare not.

DUKE of FLORENCE
How?

DOMITILLA
You dare not be so wicked I am am sure
When you remember, what you are, a Prince.

DUKE of FLORENCE

Is it a sinne for Princes to love Madam?

DOMITILLA
Or if you could dispence with so much passion
To love me, and durst give me, what I tremble
To thinke you promise, that, that very act
In which you most advance affection to me,
Would make me thinke you love me not.

DUKE of FLORENCE
Be clearer.

DOMITILLA
How should I thinke his courtship worth my trust,
And meete him with a reall change of hearts,
Who in his very first attempt of love,
Would blast my honour, and betray me to
A shame, blacke as the tongue of infamy.

DUKE of FLORENCE
Would I?

DOMITILLA
And more;
For you in this
Would tempt me to an act, by which I should
Not onely wound my selfe to death of honour,
But make me guilty of anothers blood,
And kill an innocent Lady, whose least teare
Is worth a thousand lives of perjurd men
That make a scorne of vertue.

DUKE of FLORENCE
What Lady?

DOMITILLA
Have you forgot the Princesse Sir?

DUKE of FLORENCE
The Princesse!

DOMITILLA
In that name youle finde your selfe agen
Lost in a mist of passions; oh thinke
The fames and hopes of two rich countries are
Engag'd upon your faith; your highnesse pardon,
I finde some blushes chide my too much boldnesse,
And by a nearer view now of your goodnesse,

I see my errour to beleeve you meant
Other then triall of me, or could fall
To any thought beneath your birth and honour.

DUKE of FLORENCE
But if Theodosia be made anothers
By her owne gift, and I at large, with what
Justice may I be thought then to addresse
My passions hither.

DOMITILLA
If the Princesse, which
I must not thinke, give your heart backe agen,
And that you could quit all your tyes with honour,
My thoughts are all resign'd to the Kings will;
He must dispose of me, by my owne vow,
Without his free conlent never to marry.

[Exit.

DUKE of FLORENCE
The King; there tis; I thought shee was his mistresse;
Tis not possible the Princesse now
Can pardon my neglect; Montaltoes practise
Vpon me, and his poysoning of her vertue
Wo'not excuse my shame; I dare not see
Whom I have injur'd, Theodosia;
In am resolv'd, this night Ile leave from Naples.

[Enter **THEODOSIA**.

THEODOSIA
Nay doe not hide your face my Lord; it will
Appeare as fresh and lovely to my eyes,
As when it first presented me your smiles;
I am Theodosia still.

DUKE of FLORENCE
But I have beene?

THEODOSIA
Abus'd; time will discover to the ruine
Of his owne name, and glory of our loves,
Montaltoes practise to divide our sonles.

DUKE of FLORENCE
You cannot be so mercifull; or else
This sweetnefle is put on to enlarge my guilt,

When we are both compar'd; dare you beleeve
I can repent and be'reveng'd.

THEODOSIA
Upon whom?

DUKE of FLORENCE
Upon my selfe, for suffering my eyes
To wander from this sweetnesse.

THEODOSIA
You outdoe
The satisfaction; if your grace can finde
Me grow agen within your heart, where first
My love desired to plant.

DUKE of FLORENCE
Oh let me drowne
My blushes in this over slow of charity;
But there's an act that justice calls me to,
Before I can be worthy of this peace.
Montalto has plaid the villaine; now I finde it,
And from his treacherous heart my sword must force
A bloody satisfaction for thy honour,
Poyson'd by him.

THEODOSIA
Stay that revenge; shame has
Already sunke him.

[Enter a **COURTIER**.

COURTIER
Sir the King desires
Some conference with your grace, and with you Madam.

THEODOSIA
I shall attend you Sir; we shall present
Together, thus no object to displese him.

DUKE of FLORENCE
Though I shall blush to see him, Ile waite on you.

[Exeunt.

SCENE II

Another Room in the Scene.

[Enter **KING of NAPLES, RIVIERO, ANDRUGIO**; **PETITIONERS,** who deliver their petitions to the **KING and** exeunt.

KING of NAPLES
Good heaven, upon what humane bosome shall
We that are made your substitutes on earth
Place secure confidence? and yet there may
Be malice in complaints; the flourishing Oake
For his extent of Branches, stature, growth,
The darling and the Idoll of the wood,
Whose awefull nod the under trees adore,
Shooke by a tempest, and throwne downe must needs
Submit his curled head and full growne limbes,
To every common Axe, be patient, while
The tortures put to every joynt the Sawes
And engines, making with their very noyse
The Forrests groane and tremble; but not one
When it was in his strength and state revil'd it,
Whom poverty of soule, and envy sends
To gather stickes from the trees wish'd for rume,
The great mans Embleme; I did love Montalto,
And wed not have him lost if justice would
Consent, and be a little of his side;
But here are the two plummets weigh him downe;
His impious practice on the Duke, and base
Aspertions on our sister that defame
Our whole blood, is a loud, loud accusation.

RIVIERO
His conscience dares not Sir deny't.

KING of NAPLES
And you
Speake here the tragicke story of Riviero,
Whose honest soule for not complying with
His power and ends, chose in a discontent
To make himselfe an exile, yee pursude,
And by the practise of Montalto poyson'd
At Rome.

ANDRUGIO
This letter sent to Alvarez,
Whose treacherous Physicke purg'd his soule away,
Is too much testimony.

KING of NAPLES
Tis his Character.

[Enter **OCTAVIO**.

Octavio you come for justice too.

OCTAVIO
It were a vaine breath to desire it Sir;
Your thoughts are still so conscious of vertue,
They will prevent petition.

KING of NAPLES
Come nearer.

RIVIERO
The King is troubled.

ANDRUGIO
Where he loved, to finde
So much ingratitude.

KING of NAPLES
Andrugio.

RIVIERO
Things are not yet mature for my discovery.

KING of NAPLES
You observe—away—

[Exit **ANDRUGIO**

OCTAVIO
We may be just Philoberto,
Yet not destroy another attribute,
Which shewes whose repre sentative we are;
Mercy becomes a King; too much can be
But thought a sinne on the right hand; we are
Resolv'd.

[Enter **SIMPHORSA**.

Madam you are welcome.

RIVIERO
I begin
To feare there is some spell upon the King;

If after this Montalto shall prevaile,
Let innocence be stronger to the world,
And heaven be afraid to punish vice.

KING of NAPLES
Remove
For a few minuts.

RIVIERO
I obey.

[Exit.

KING of NAPLES
You tell me wonders Madam; las poore Lady,
I shall then have enough to reconcile;
Shee was too hasty to interpret me
Her lover.

SIMPHOROSA
If you Sir apply no cure,
The fond impression may I feare indanger
Her sence and life; I urg'd Montalto Sir
By your command, before his change of fortune,
But shee tooke no delight to heare him named.

KING of NAPLES
No, no, nor I; good heaven how I am troubled
How to repaire this pretty peece of innocence,
Whom I have brought into a waking dreame
Of passion; something I must doe; pray tell me,
But tell me truth; I charge thee by thy duty
To me, to Naples, and to heaven, or if
There be in womans faith, or thy Religion
Any thing else to make it up a full
And perfect conjuration.

SIMPHOROSA
You fright me;
Without these not a thought within my heart
But you have power to summon.

KING of NAPLES
Tell me then,
Is Domitilla vertuous?

SIMPHOROSA
How Sir?

KING of NAPLES
Is shee exceeding vertuous; is shee most
Divinely chast; can shee doe more then blush
At wanton sounds; will shee be'very angry
At an immodest offer, and be frighted
To heare it nam'd; tell me; does shee pray
And weepe, and wod be torne upon the racke
Ere shee consent to staine one virgin thought:
Or dares shee more then Lucrece kill her selfe
To save her honour, or doe something more
Miraculously then all this to preserve
Her white name to posterity.

SIMPHOROSA
I know not
How to reply to these particulars;
But if your meaning be to have me speake
Truth of her modest and pare thoughts, shee is
All that her mother can beseech of heaven
To blesse a childe with of so chast a soule,
And vertuous simplicity.

KING of NAPLES
No more;
I doe beleeve, and will finde out a way
To make her satisfaction; tis just;
Say I desire her presence.

SIMPHOROSA
Now you blesse us;
A widdowes prayers and teares for this great bounty.

[Exit.

[Enter **RIVIERO**.

RIVIERO
Your sister and the Duke Sit.

KING of NAPLES
There's new trouble.

RIVIERO
Never so lovingly united;
The pleasant language of their eyes and gestutes
Doth speake their hearts at peace.

KING of NAPLES
That would rejoyce me.

[Exit **RIVIERO**.

[Enter **DUKE of FLORENCE, THEODOSIA**.

THEODOSIA
Take us to your love;
All jealousies are banish'd, and we both
Breath from one soule.

KING of NAPLES
My wonder and my joy.

DUKE of FLORENCE
Your pardon.

KING of NAPLES
Take my bosome.

THEODOSIA
The misfortune
Kept us at distance, was your creatures act.

KING of NAPLES
The clouds are now remov'd.

RIVIERO
Lord Montalto, Sir.

KING of NAPLES
Let Musicke speake
His deare approach; we sent for him.

RIVIERO
How's this:

KING of NAPLES
Let me intreate you to obscute your persons
A while.

[Exit **DUKE of FLORENCE, THEODOSIA**.

[Loud Musicke—Enter **GUIDO, ALOISIO, ALEXIO, ANDRUGIO, OCTAVIO, MONTALTO**.

KING of NAPLES
My Lord y'are welcome to us, very welcome

We have kept our word, and finde you have not lost
Your confidence; what a brave armour is
An innocent soule? How like a rocke it bids
Defiance to a storme, against whose ribbes
The insolent waves, but dash themselves in peeces,
And fall and hide their heads in passionate foam!
How would a guilty person tremble now,
Looke pale, and with his eyes chain'd to the ground
Betray his feare of justice.

MONTALTO
Where should honour
Shine with his pure and native luistre, but
Where there is such a King, so good, so great,
The example and reward; he must be
A rebell twice to virtue that can live
To be convinc'd of a dishonour neare
Such an instructive goodnesse.

KING of NAPLES
Where be all his fierce accusets?
Call 'em to his presence,
Whom all their envies would destroy.

RIVIERO
So, so;
The King is charm'd [aside].

OCTAVIO
They are gone upon the first
Newes of my Lords return they vanish'd Sir.

MONTALTO
So may all reason fly the brow of innocence.

KING of NAPLES
Tis well said; but they sha not fly their names;
Reade there just to our thoughts, they apprehended
Thee lost in our displeasure (wheres our sister)
And now they came to be reveng'd Montalto,
Upon our favours.

GUIDO
Right, and please your grace.

KING of NAPLES
Theres something may concerne your want of grace
Andrugio, Philoberto.

[Gives them papers.

MONTALTO
We are undone Guido, and I see more
Engines are leveld at my fate.

RIVIERO
The King would have your Lordship peruse this.

ANDRUGIO
And these.

[They give the papers to **MONTALTO**, who reads them.

RIVIERO
That you may know your friends and enemies.

MONTALTO
Lost, lost for ever.

RIVIERO
Sir you know
You have obliged the Princesse Theodosia
And the Duke to you, and you may presume
To use their favours, they are here.

[Enter **DUKE of FLORENCE**, **THEODOSIA**.

MONTALTO
Twere better
For me they had no beeing. I did never
Expect this; to accuse me for the death
Of Riviero; but I must obey
This fatall revolution.

[Kneels.

KING of NAPLES
Why does Montalto kneele.

MONTALTO
I dare not aske your pardon,
Onely I beg you would put on a brow
Rough as the cause you have to make it frowne,
And that may strike me dead without more torment.

KING of NAPLES

Ingratefull man! am I rewarded thus.
Not onely with my faith abus'd and subjects,
But wounding all our honours.

THEODOSIA
Let him finde your mercy Sir
For his offence to me.

[Enter **SIMPHOROSA, DOMITILLA**.

KING of NAPLES
I must not, dare not pardon; twere a sinne
In me of violence to heaven and justice.

MONTALTO
You have beene a Royall Master.

KING of NAPLES
Take him hence;
His life will draw a scorne upon the Kingdome;
Expect the censure of our lawes you gentlemen,
We onely banish from the court.

GUIDO, ALOISIO, ALEXIO
You are mercifull.

KING of NAPLES
Pray and be honest.

RIVIERO
That last will be the greatest penance to them.

KING of NAPLES
My passion would be strong but here is one
Come to divert the streame; how is it with
My pretty Domitilla; you and I
May change some words in private.

[Takes **DOMITILLA** aside.

OCTAVIO
The King is just, and tis within your silence
To make Montalto nothing.

RIVIERO
Hee will sinke
Apace without that weight upon him; malice
Shall have no share in my revenge.

KING of NAPLES
And since Montalto
Is become incapable,
I wo'not marry thee; that's a thing too common?
But thou shalt be my mistresse, a preferment
Above my first intention; be wise
And entertaine it; oh the dayes and nights
Weele spend together!

OCTAVIO
The King's very pleasant
With Domitilla.

KING of NAPLES
Come kisse me
Domitilla; kisse me now
Before all these; what needs this modesty?
Come let us take in one anothers soule.

DOMITILLA
Are you the King of Naples.

KING of NAPLES
So they call me,
And if there be a power within that name
It shall be thine to make thee glorious,
And great above our Queene; there is no title
Like unto that our heate and blood creates—
A mistresse Domitilla.

DOMITILLA
Are you Sir in earnest?

KING of NAPLES
Doe but thou consent, and I
Will give thee such a proofe in my embraces
Of the delight; they will not follow us;
I'll tell thee more i'th bed-chamber.

DOMITILLA
I dare
Not understand this language can the King
Be impious; how was my opinion cozen'd
Sinne hath deform'd his very shape; his voyce
Hath now no harmony.

KING of NAPLES

This is but to draw
More courtship from me.

DOMITILLA
Pardon I beseech you;
I have found my errour.

KING of NAPLES [aside]
Will shee yeeld?

DOMITILLA
I did consent
Too soone to my captivity,
Though modesty would not allow me strength
To tell you so; but you have Sir, by what
My fond thoughts never did expect, reliev'd me,
to make me know my selfe; and now preserving
That duty which I owe you as my King,
I call love backe agen, and can looke on
Your lusts with a becomming scorne.

KING of NAPLES
You can.

DOMITILLA
Yes, and were Naples, Rome, and all the wealth
Of Italy laid downe, the great temptation,
Thus I would spurne their glories.

KING of NAPLES
Come this is but the tricke of all your sex;
We know you can dissemble appetite,
As if you were not slesh and blood.

DOMITILLA
Sir give
Me leave to goe while I have power to pray for you,
Where was I lost? is there no friend to goodnesse;
Have I contracted such a leprous forme
That I have lost all mens defence and charity.

OCTAVIO
Madam your innocence doth raise in me,
Though young, a willing champion, and with
My safe obedience to the King, I dare,
Armde with the witnesse of her cause, defie
The greatest souldier in the world.

KING of NAPLES
How's this?

OCTAVIO
Sir, in a noble canse, if you to whom
In the first place truth flies as to an Altar,
Wave her religious defence I dare dye for her.

KING of NAPLES
You so brave? to prison with him;
We will correct your saucinesse.

OCTAVIO
You will grace
My first act Sir, and get me same by suffering
For so much sweetnesse.

DOMITILLA
Let not your displeasure
Great Sir fall upon him; revenge what you
Call disobedience here.

KING of NAPLES
You owe much to
His confidence; nor is there any punishment
Beyond your love and liking of his boldnesse;
You two should make a marriage with your follies.

OCTAVIO
Let Domitilla make Octavio
So blest.

DOMITILLA
My Lord you now deserve I should
Be your's, whom with the hazard of the Kings
Anger, and your owne life you have defended;
There is a spring of honour here, and too it
In the presence of the King, his Court and Heaven,
I dare now give my heart; nor is't without
My duty to a promise.

OCTAVIO
Now you make
Octavio happy.

KING of NAPLES
Tis to my desires,
And I dare wish you joyes; forgive this practise;

—Nay preety Domitilla I did this
But to divert more happily thy thoughts
Of me, who have not paide yet the full tribute
To my my Cesarias dust; agen let me
Congratulate thy choise in young Octavio,
Whose birth and forward vertue will deserve thee;
Brother and sister love, and wish them happinesse.

THEODOSIA
May all joyes spring within their hearts.

DUKE of FLORENCE
I must present this gentleman to be more knowne to you

OCTAVIO
I hope you are no enemy to this blessing.

SIMPHOROSA
I adde what doth become a most glad mother, blessing to your loves.

KING of NAPLES
Noble Riviero.

RIVIERO
I live agen by your acknowledgment.

DUKE of FLORENCE
Sir you may trust my testimony; Alvarez
Letter is now an argument of his safety,
Who is yet living to increase the guilt
Of false Montalto.

KING of NAPLES
Welcome; tis thy life
That hath revers'd Montaltoes doome, whose sentence
Now shall bee onely banishment; our hearts
Are full and sprightly; nothing wants but to
Perfect with holy ceremony, what
Your hearts have seal'd; mirth in each bosome flowes,
Distraction never had so sweet a close.

[Exeunt.

THE EPILOGUE

As it was spoken to the Lord Deputie on Newyeares-day at night, by way of vote, congratulating the New yeare.

Our Poet doth forget his Play;
There is something he would pay
Due to your greatnesse, and the day
Which by a revolution of the spheare
Is proud to open the New yeare.
And having look'd on you, hath hid his face,
And Chang'd his robe with Starres to grace
And light you going to bed, so waite
With trembling Lustre on your state.
Shine brighter yet, y'are not the same
Cleare Lampes you were shine like the name
Of him I bow too, while aflame
Active, and burning here with pure desires
Shall equall the best borrowed fires.
May health, the bosomes friend, streame through your blood,
And know no ebbe of the chast flood,
And though time shift, and yeares renew,
May yet the Spring be still in you.
May She, whom heaven hath sweetly grac'd
And in your noble bosome plac'd,
Whose heart by onely yours embrac'd,
Hath made one true, and holy Gordian, prove
Fruitfull in Children, as in love.
And may this faire Top-branch, whose early bloome
Doth promise all the fruit can come
To vertue, and your name be blest,
And live a story to the rest.
All Honour with your fame in crease,
In your bosome dwell soft peace,
And Iustice, the true roote of these;
Wealth be the worst, and out side of your fate;
And may not heaven your life translate,
Till for your Royall Master, and this Ile,
Your deeds have fild a Chronicle,
In all thats great, and good, be bold,
And every yeare be coppie of the old.

FINIS

POEMS IN PRAISE OF JAMES SHIRLEY

To My Ingenious Friend, James Shirley, Upon His Royall Master by James Mervyn

As a rich gemme enchac'd in gold affords
More radiant lustre to the gazers eye
Inprison'd so, within it selfe it hoords
Vp all the beamy treasures of the skie,
Beames loose reflex on bodies diaphane
But cast on solids they rebound againe,
So would thy lines my Friend in paper pent
Contract the whole applauses of the age,
But should they a neglected ornament
Be soly made the study of the Stage,
They might like water in the Sunshine set
Retaine his image, not impart his heate.
Then Print thy Poem Shirley, 'twere a fault
To dungion this instructive peece of thine,
Had the Sunnes Spheare beene made a thicke rib'd vault,
We had receiv'd no influence from his shine;
Thou shouldst die traitour to succeeding times,
And thy best vertues prove but splendid crimes.

On Mr. James Shirley's Royall Master by Fra. Butler

Such curious eyes as in a Poeme looke
For the most part, doe finde the printed booke
With verses frontispic'd, to shew their wit
In praise of the authors which occasions it,
And I have seene some peeces, that have stood
In neede of witnesses to prove them good.
This Poets skill is here so clearely showne
In offering light to his they dimme their owne,
For all that with unsquinted eyes shall see
This well limb'd pecce of polish'd poesie,
In justice to themselves must needes confesse
Friends cannot adde, nor envie make it lesse.

Upon Mr. James Shirley His Comedy, Cal'd The Royall Master by Drv. Cooper

When Spencer reign'd sole Prince of Poets here,
As by his Fairy Queene doth well appeare
There was not one so blind, so bold a Bard,
So ignorantly proud or foolish-hard
To encounter his sweete Muse; for Phoebus vow'd
A sharp: revenge on him should be so proud;
And when my Shirley from the Albion shore
Comes laden with the Muses, all their store

Transferres to Dublin, full Parnassus brings,
And all the riches of Castalian Springs;
Shall we not welcome him with our just votes?
And shall we doo't with harsh and envious notes?
No no, Thalia, Envy shall not sit
So high above our judgement, and our wit,
As not to give just merit his due praise,
And crowne thy Poet with deserved Bayes.
Shirley stand forth, and put thy Lawrell on,
Phoebus next heire, now Ben is dead and gone,
Truly legitimate, Ireland is so just
To say, you rise the Phenix of his dust,
And since thy Royall Master won so much
On each Iudicious and hath stood the touch,
Tis fit he should more then private, when
He weares two Crownes, their votes, and thy smooth penne.

On the Royall Master, to His Friend the Author by Ric. Belling

Smooth and unsullied lines, keepe on your way,
From envies loss'le free, a cleare ey'd day
Smiles on your triumph; onely thus to blame,
Too lavish is your sacrifice to fame.
Lesse of such perfume, to succeeding age,
The dead would sweeten, and enbalme the Stage;
Here is a pile of incense, every line
Heapes on fresh Narde, your Muse cannot decline
To intermissions, some leave hills, by turnes
Flame, and expire his Etna ever burnes.

To My Deserving Friend Mr. James Shirley on His Royall Master by T.I.

I like some petty Brooke scarse worth a name,
Must yet pay tribute to thy full-stream'd fame,
But Ile not strive, (as men sometimes) to raise
An uncouth structure to thy merits praise
From others ruines, thy just minde will scorne
To owne Encomiums so basely borne.
Therefore I write, what may become my free
Acknowledgment, and fit thy modestie.

Thy Muse I honor'd, e're I knew by sight
Thy person; oft I've seene with much delight
Thy sweete composures: but this last; and new

Smooth peece (which here hath grac'd the publicke view)
Claimes more regard; I give to all the rest
Their faire desert, but ranke this with thy best.

To His Much Esteemed Friend Mr. James Shirley, on His Royall Master by W. Markham

You who the readers are of the choice wit,
And have the leading voice in censuring it,
Whose votes Grand jurors are, and onely have
The well knowne power either to kill or save,
Give this a noble greeting and its due,
May Phoebus else, withdraw his beames from you.
My worthy Friend, this Play 'oth publicke Stage
Hath gain'd such faire applause, as 't did engage
A nation to thy Muse, where thou shalt raigne
Vicegerent to Apollo, who doth daigne
(His darling Ben deceased) thou should'st be
Declar'd the heire apparant to his tree.

To the Honour'd Author of the Royall Master by W. Smith

Deare Friend I joy my love hath found the meanes
To waite upon, and vindicate thy scenes
From some few scruples of the weaker sex,
Whose nicer thoughts their female minds perplex.
(For man he sinkes if he but censure, none
Dare deprave Kings Inauguration)
Say they, what makes the King in his dispose
So Icy-temperd, as he frankly throwes
Freedome on all except himselfe? Contrives.
The way for other men a purchase wives?
Takes joy to forward propagation,
By Nuptiall knot, yet to himselfe ties none?
Prettie poore fooles, and Virgins! how you'r kind
(Vulgar like) are in apprehension blind;
Come reade, you'le see when you this peece peruse
The Royall Masters Spouse is Shirlies Muse;
Why then to him, and her, an altar raise,
Tapers are set, flaming with equall praise
See, see, his Genius gracefully doth bend
To the just vote of every loving friend;
The elevated Circle is upheld
Betwixt the binall Cherubs palmes, beheld
By all judicious eyes; the heart, the voice

Of all ingenious doe applaud the choice
Of your great Royall Master, say, they'ue found
Two Monarkes with one glorious Laurell crownd.

To His Worthy Friend the Author by John Ogleby Oglebye

All these thy friends subscribing to thy praise
And faire deservings, have done well, 'twill raise
Opinion in the readers, and engage
Them to peruse, what wee saw on the Stage.
If knowing ones, their judgement thus will be
The Commondation's short, the Comedy
Speakes better for it selfe, more home; but yet
My vote must goe, I say no purer wit
Did ever grace the scene, nay 'it hath in't
Expressions of so new, and rich a Mint,
That the old Poets well might wish the name
Of this new Play were added to their fame.

To the Much Honoured, James Shirley Upon His Royall Master by John Jacson

Let no man thinke, I hither coldly came
On purpose to commend, or to seeke fame
By this impression, that world may say,
What is this Iackson that commends the play?
Though tis a grace, to stand as Courtiers use
To usher in the reader to thy Muse,
Yet by the way, Ile tell him I have read
The Lawes of Flaccus with a serious head,
And that according to those statutes there
(Never to be repeal'd) thy Poems are,
Thy discreete stile is elegantly plaine,
In Sock and Buskin, proper to each veine
Of Time, Place, Person, and that all thy wit
Is not by chance but regularly writ;
Nor dost thou gall the Theater, we may
Be acted every man, yet see thy play
Invisible, so curious is thy Pen
Which can at once, would heale, and better men,
Therefore will I hereafter cease to mourne
For those great wits, commended to the Vrne,
And if't be true, that transmigrations be
They are in Shirley all, for ought I see.

On M. James Shirley His Royall Master by James Mervyn

There are some men doe hold, there is a place
Cal'd Limbus Patrum if such have the grace
To wave that Schisme, and Poetarum said
They of that saith had me a member made,
That Limbus I could have beleev'd thy braine
Where Beamont, Fletcher, Shakespeare, & a traine
Of glorious Poets in their active heate
Move in that Orbe, as in their former seate.
When thou began'st to give thy Master life,
Me thought I saw them all, with friendly strife
Each casting in his dose, Beamont his weight,
Shakespeare his mirth, and Fletcher his conceit,
With many more ingredients, with thy skill
So sweetely tempered, that the envious quill
And tongue of Critricks must both write and say,
They never yet beheld a smoother Play.

www.ingramcontent.com/pod-product-compliance
Lightning Source LLC
Chambersburg PA
CBHW071305040426
42444CB00009B/1879